Life, Lemons and Melons

By Alice-May Purkiss

Illustrated by Georgia Wilmot

A note on this book.

I am a person who has had cancer.
I am a person who has depression.
It is not my intention to speak for all people
who have lived through these experiences.

This book is purely based on my experience.
I'm not an expert.
I'm just a person who wants to make sure
anyone who ever finds themselves
in either of these boats never feels
like they're alone.

I'm not speaking for you.
I'm speaking for me.
But I hope the experiences I share in the following
pages can be a light in the dark if you're
looking for one.

Thanks for reading

xx

It's kind of hard to know where to begin.

If, like me, you've grown up with a life centred around musicals or Disney movies, word is that it's best to start at the very beginning. But when I think about the "beginning" of this story, I look at it as if it's through some kind of weird mirror. This mirror distorts the things that happened before I knew the story had begun, making me question what was actually the very start. Events that unfurled in the months before, with hindsight now appear angular and stilted. They're covered by a weird film of knowledge. When I look at photographs of that time, the time before 7th July 2015, especially the events in the weeks just before when I was, unbeknown to me, carrying around something that was about to change my life, if not forever, then definitely for the next year or so, it's like looking at a stranger.

When I think about the person I was then, I wonder how I would have felt if I had known what was to come. I wonder if I would have been afraid or if I would have closed myself off from the world. I wonder if the darkness I was so used to living in would have taken me completely. Had I known, had I known.

I've thought a lot about why I wanted to write this book over the months I have been writing it. When I started blogging about my experience of cancer, I did it for mainly selfish reasons. I wanted an outlet in which to disentangle my thoughts. But my blog became a place for other people to hang out too. It offered support and a community for other young people with breast cancer. And it became a safe place for me to be honest. It started a conversation that was different from the one directed at older women, that I had felt so far removed from.

With this book though, the thing you are actually holding in your hands, I wanted to let people know they are not alone. I wanted to offer Albus Dumbledore's light in the dark - not necessarily to insist things will get better, because I know that's not necessarily what you want to hear - but to remind people that the human race knows a thing or two about both suffering and survival, and with that in mind, it's more difficult to feel totally isolated in your struggles - whether they're related to mental health or cancer, or something completely different. Someone has been where you are right now. And while that doesn't make your shitty situation any less shitty, it suggests that survival is possible. Even if it's just surviving one day at a time. One moment at a time. You've made it through every single one of your bad days until now - you can take whatever life throws at you. We are surviving even when we are just living today and that is enough.

So where do we begin?

I suppose, like with most things in life, the defining points blur. There isn't really a beginning, a middle and an end. There are just a collection of events that unfurled around me, largely out of my control, and I just kind of bumbled along with them. If there's one thing I have learned in the last three years it is that there's not much in life we are in control of. The universe has it's own plans for you and you've just gotta roll with them, appreciating that the world is not out to get you, even when it feels like it might be.

But regardless of who is in control of the events that unfolded in the latter part of my twenties, perhaps ones which were set in motion much longer ago, it's not clear where to begin with telling you about them all. You might find that there are certain parts of this book that come in an order you don't expect them to - it's definitely told in a very non-sequential fashion. I think part of the reason for this is because there's a lot I didn't process in a linear fashion. There's no real beginning, or middle or end. And the brain doesn't tend to work in a linear fashion either. Or mine doesn't at any rate, and that's the brain I'm working with. Shall we dive in?

Chapter 1: Diagnosis

It's a fairly sunny Tuesday in July. It's actually the tenth anniversary of the 7/7 terrorist attacks on London. Ten years since 52 people were killed and over 770 were injured when bombs were set off across the London transport network. Both buses and tubes were affected. But you know all this.

I'm sat with Chris, my long-suffering boyfriend of almost ten years in a waiting room at Lewisham Hospital in South East London. There's a memorial service on the television for all those who lost their lives on that horrible day in 2005. I watch the second hand on the clock to the right of the television screen tick slowly around. We've been sat here for a while, but neither of us really mind. We both agree that complaining about the NHS is like complaining that your sports car doesn't run well enough. It kind of makes you look like a bit of a jerk. We are privileged to be sat here, waiting for the expert doctors to see us without having to worry about insurance or finances or anything like that. We are both grateful for the incredible healthcare we have at our fingertips.

My boyfriend is tapping away on his phone. I'm trying desperately to concentrate on reading *The Goldfinch* by Donna Tartt, determined to finish it soon. I'm obsessed with the amount of books we read in our lifetime and this one, as good as it is, has been slowing me down. I keep getting distracted by the other people in the room. There are barely any empty seats. The clinic is busy and bustling despite the memorial two minutes' silence that is unfolding on the telly in front of us. Nurses sporadically appear and summon people to follow them. Men and women. A range of ages.

I'm wearing a Hogwarts t-shirt with high-waisted jeans and battered trainers. I realise I'm dressed a bit like a child. My hair has been thrown up into a half ponytail-bun thing that makes me look a bit like I'm attempting to do my best impression of a Star-Trek based android. It's the longest it has been for years after I lopped off my bottom-length hair into a pixie cut in one fell swoop when I was 18. I wear a heavy block fringe. There's the very, very slightest hint of pink on the ends - a hangover from another year at Glastonbury festival.

I should probably re-wind a little bit.

***

A few months earlier in May, as I'm getting ready for work, my hand brushes against something unusual in my right breast. I'm in the habit of checking myself regularly, but this wasn't even one of the regular rendezvous I have with my breasts around once a month.

I have a bit of a prod around and think it feels a bit like a lump. A very, very small lump, but a lump nonetheless. I call to my boyfriend.

"Erm. Babes. Weird question. Would you mind coming and having a look at my boob for a second?"

Never one to look a gift horse in the mouth, he obviously obliges and gives my right knocker a bit of an "examination".

"I can't feel anything" he says. "Just keep an eye on it and see what you think, but it's probably just muscular or hormonal or something."

I nod in agreement and carry on with my day, not really giving it a second thought. To be honest, I kind of forget about it completely.

I'm working full time as a social media manager for an online company that's going through a lot of changes and I'm focusing most of my energy on that. I barely have time to think about what I'm going to have for dinner, let alone a mysterious lump that's probably just going to be a cyst or something.

A week or so passes and I'm in Cornwall. I've thrown myself into a staycation with what can only be described as "aplomb" - surfing in the bracing sea on the shores of the stunning Fistral Beach. climbing through history at Tintagel, taking Cornish tea on the Lizard heritage coast. We visit the tropics of the Eden Project, trek to St Michael's Mount and lose ourselves in the Gardens of Helligan. In the modern world, carrying a computer around in your pocket with you 24 hours a day, seven days a week, often limits the amount of space we allow ourselves. Pulled from London to a place with patchy phone signal and an incredibly limited internet connection, I find myself more in the moment than I've been for quite some time.

It's then that the memory of this lump pervades my life again, this time as I'm going about having a bloody brilliant holiday in bloody brilliant Britain. My hand brushes past my right breast as I'm taking a shower. This time I know I feel something.

Back at home, I plan to make an appointment to see the doctor, but with life being as busy as it often is in London and with work as manic as it has been, I don't do it as quickly as I should. I mention to my Mum that I found a little lump and she begins (rightly so) yammering on at me about going to the doctors and getting it checked out. "But I can't get an appointment" I insist, even though I haven't tried particularly hard. "I've got loads of stuff on this week, Mum" I tell her, "I just don't have time to go to the doctors." Her voice becomes hard and stern. She's pulling the

Mum act on me.

"Alice-May Purkiss". Oh god. She has full-named me. She means business. "You call the doctors right now. You tell them you have a lump in your breast and that you need to be seen."

I roll my eyes unfairly, thinking she's making a big deal about nothing, *telling* myself she's making a big deal about nothing. Nevertheless, I make an appointment to see my GP the next day. I know that she'll be calling me to chase up whether I have or not and I decide it is not worth the earful if I haven't done it already.

The young male registrar I'm greeted by at the surgery seems almost embarrassed by my willingness to let him have a feel of my knockers without a chaperone present. A few years previously, I'd had a fibroadenoma (a benign lump made up of fibrous and glandular tissue) removed from my left breast, so I felt pretty casual about the whole thing. As unconfident as I am in real life, and as few people have seen my boobs in the outside world, baring myself to medical practitioners never really seems to be much of an issue. I very much assume I'll be told this is the same thing and sent on my way. He actually tells me he thinks it is a breast mouse - a non-cancerous breast lump that can be moved around within the breast tissue. **But** he decides to send me to the experts at Lewisham Hospital breast clinic anyway. I leave the surgery, feeling pretty pleased with myself. I've swerved getting another telling off from my Mother. No-one likes to be full-named by their Mother, whether you're four or 34.

Less than two weeks pass. An appointment to go to the breast clinic drops through the letterbox. I pop along, still feeling largely blasé about this pesky little lump hanging around in the side of my right breast. The surgeon I see tells me he's pretty sure that, given that I'm only 26, it's probably nothing sinister. He says he is 95% certain that "this is not a bad lump". I think you can see what's coming here. The chances of it not being a bad lump were probably more like 99%, but he'd rounded down. There probably really was a less than 5% chance of it being a bad lump. Probably less than 1% in reality. According to Cancer Research, 9 out of 10 breast lumps are benign, and combined with my age, general wellbeing and lack of family history, it looked incredibly unlikely.

But, to be on the safe side he decides to send me down to the imaging department for an ultrasound scan and to get a biopsy anyway.

There are two buts in the three preceding paragraphs. Both of these buts are incredibly important in my story. Had it not been for those two buts, we could have been looking at a distinctly different narrative to the one that unfolded after that date. I am eternally grateful for both of those buts. And I'm incredibly grateful that the systems the NHS has in place and the care of the staff both at my GP's surgery and at the breast clinic were so effective that I wasn't failed.

Now let me carry on and stop thinking about butts, OK? Where was I? Oh yes.

I meander down to the imaging suite. I'm more concerned about the fact that the last time I was in a hospital, I held my Grandmother's hand as she died in front of me, rather than the lump I'm having investigated. Hospitals have always made me uncomfortable and that day only cemented the fact that I hate everything about them.

Once again, I whap my baps out without a second thought. A

radiologist squirts jelly on my boob and begins to ultrasound the whole thing. I see the images on the screen. The lump is blatantly clear on the screen. I naively say to the very nice radiologist "Blimey. Is that the lump I can feel? Science is JUST incredible, isn't it?" She nods, doesn't say very much in response. She gets right up in my lymph nodes. I find this a little bit uncomfortable. Possibly more so than lying in front of a stranger with my boobs out.

"Have you been unwell recently at all?" she asks me, still fixing her gaze determinedly on the screen that one usually associates with seeing babies on the telebox (unless, I suppose, you've had a baby yourself, then you probably associate it with that). I say nope. I'm in rude health, I think to myself. The fittest I've ever been, the healthiest I've ever been. I'm actually feeling pretty bloody well, I think to myself, apart from the fact I have this inexplicable lump in my breast. The radiologist mentions that my lymph nodes are a bit inflamed and this is usually linked to an infection.

She takes a biopsy. It's a bit like being stapled in the chest.

I leave the hospital and make my way into work. I am bruised and a bit confused but generally feeling pretty chipper. I speak to my Mum on the phone again to tell her they took a biopsy. I mention that my lymphs were swollen. She goes a bit quiet. I clamour to make her feel better, telling her a tiny fib that I've been feeling a bit ropey for a couple of weeks and I'm probably just fighting off an infection. I tell her they'll post my results in two weeks. She doesn't seem placated, but we hang up and both go about our days.

I Google what swollen lymph nodes could mean.

"Glands can also swell following an injury, such as a cut or bite, near the gland or when a tumor or infection occurs in the mouth, head, or neck. Glands in the armpit (axillary lymph nodes) may swell from an injury or infection to the arm or hand. A rare cause of axillary swelling may be breast cancer or lymphoma."

Cool, I think to myself. Probably just an infection. Probably nothing. Won't be breast cancer. I'm only 26. What a silly thought.

Two weeks later, I get a call from a breast care nurse at the hospital. Her name is Varna. She is kind and friendly. She tells me that the surgeon would like to see me. She offers me an appointment in ten days' time. I tell her I'll be in Menorca then. She offers me an appointment for the day after tomorrow. I tell her I'll be at Glastonbury then. She tells me it seems like I have a pretty great fortnight planned. I agree, tell her I've been waiting all year for this to roll around. She tells me she needs to check something with the surgeon, pops me on hold, then comes back and makes an appointment with me for when I get back. 11am on 7/7/15.

I tell her I look forward to seeing her then. I tell her to have a lovely day. She tells me to have a lovely fortnight.

I'm starting to get a bit concerned.

Somehow, I manage to lose myself for five hedonistic days at Glastonbury Festival as I dance my way through the fields of the best place on Earth. I watch Kasabian, Ben Howard and Hot Chip. I bemoan the distinct lack of the Foo Fighters after Dave Grohl (there goes my hero) broke his leg a few weeks prior to the festival. 90% of the time, I manage to put the impending hospital appointment to the back of my mind. But for 10% of the time, worry creeps in. Why have I been called back to the clinic? It must just be to do more tests, I tell myself.

While we're in Menorca, doing little other than reading and eating and laughing and drinking with gorgeous friends, I manage to keep the appointment from my mind for 70% of the time.

"What if it's bad news?" I ask Chris as we stand in our room in the Menorcan villa, feeling the lump for the umpteenth time. I think it has grown. He looks at me.

"If it's bad news, we'll deal with it," he says, simply. I cannot argue with that.

***

We get back from our restorative trip to Spain on a Sunday afternoon in early July. Tuesday rolls around. Chris has taken the morning off to come with me. Just in case.

Back in the hospital, the time edges closer to noon. I glance around the room and realise that I am the youngest person in here by some margin. I think to myself how crazy it is that some people in this room are about to be told something that will change their lives for ever - that their body has turned against them and begun growing mutated cells that want to kill them. I never really expect that I could be one of those people.

At about four minutes to midday, a nurse appears, recognising me immediately. As the youngest person in the room, I suppose I stick out a bit. She introduces herself as the nurse I'd spoken to on the phone a few short weeks ago. Once again she is kind and friendly. She smiles. I like her immediately. She asks how

Glastonbury was, asks how Menorca was. I laugh and tell her I think I've had the best two weeks of my life, tell her how incredibly lucky I feel. She shows me into a consulting room, where an amiable gentleman is sat, wearing a rather impressive bow tie. I love a bow tie. I think I might even tell him I like his bow tie.

He introduces himself and looks straight at me through his large bifocal glasses.

"Miss Purkiss.

There's no easy way to say this.

The lump we biopsied is cancerous.

You have breast cancer."

I am 26 years old. I have breast cancer. My breast is trying to kill me.

How on earth do I tell my Mother?

We discuss how we will be moving forward, what will happen next. Words like surgery, triple negative, grade three, stage two B/ three are thrown around. I lose track of what is being said to me.

I want to say that my world is shattered, that I began to cry uncontrollably, that my heart breaks, like you see in the movies - but in truth, it doesn't. If anything, my heart hardens as I listen to the details of how we will proceed. Little else from that appointment sticks in my mind. I feel nothing other than Chris' hand on the small of my back. I remember nothing other than the ghostly white colour his face is when I turn to look at him for the first time since the doctor said the word "cancer."

Concerns about surgery or chemotherapy or radiotherapy don't even begin to cross my mind as I try to take in the enormity of what the surgeon is telling me. I don't cry a single tear. I go into survival mode and begin planning how I would tell all the people who needed to know.

Varna takes me into another room to take a few bloods and give me more literature about breast cancer than I can even carry. I empty out the contents of my work bag, removing the copy of *The Goldfinch*, my purse, my notebook. If I have to carry something in my arms as I leave the hospital, I would rather it was symbols of normality than the mountain of information that will identify me as a breast cancer patient to any onlookers. The nurse tells me she will be my point of contact at the hospital in the future. Anything I need, she tells me she will help me with it. She gives me her card. She tells me that it's OK to cry. I make a joke. Little do I know this is the start of my career as a cancer joker, something which will unsettle many but offers me an inordinate amount of comfort. I've always been one to try to laugh when I want to cry. Many of my stories are ones that shouldn't be funny, but in the telling of them, I make them funny. Cancer adds a whole other dimension to this aspect of my life and character.

My phone buzzes continually as my mother waits anxiously 300 miles away with my Dad and my sister, hoping to hear good news. I don't know how I am going to tell her it is not good news. My phone keeps buzzing. This time it is my sister.

"Mum is really worried. Can you call her please?"

My mum calls again and leaves a voicemail.

"Hello poppet. Just checking in. Can you let me know what happened at the hospital this morning?"

I turn my phone off. I need time to begin to figure this out before I drop the bombshell on my family. I feel an overwhelming sense of guilt about the fact I'm going to bring such an inordinate sense of stress and fear and worry. To my parents. To my sister. To my nonagenarian paternal Grandparents. A family which has only just begun to heal itself after watching my once vivacious and virile Grandmother, the matriarch of our family, fade in front of our eyes. And now we are all being faced with another reminder of our own mortality.

I tell my boss before I tell my family. I foolishly think I can put my Mum off until I can make it to the North East to tell them all in person. It's a three hour train journey to my hometown from Kings' Cross. I'm clearly not thinking straight if I think I can put them all off for that long.

The first time I say it out loud, it feels like a lie. Like a weird and twisted lie of someone who isn't completely sane. I watch as the expressions in the room change. My work colleague, who I consider a brilliant friend, takes my hand as she tries not to cry. The expressions of my managers, who don't know me as well but need to be told, switch instantly. I see the blood drain from their faces. I see their mouths drop for just a second.

I will see the face of the first person I say "I have breast cancer" out loud to for the first time for the rest of my life.

The weird thing is, I know he's reading this. I wonder if he knows he was the first person I said it to out loud. I wonder how that bombshell affected him.

I end up telling my family that I have breast cancer over the phone while sitting in a meeting room in my office, which is essentially a glass box. I was quite literally in a glass cage of emotion.

***

I suppose the only other thing to tell you at this point is that it's not only my boob that I've got problems with. My brain is a little bit broken too. About eight months before this appointment, after living the majority of my adult life in the shadows, in the tight and unrelenting grasps of a darkness that I often tried to deny, I was diagnosed with depression.

So here I am, just a few months later, in the midst of receiving cognitive behavioural therapy, taking a little tablet called Citalopram every single day, finally feeling like I've got my shit a bit more together than I ever have before and I've just been told I have a life threatening illness.

Breast cancer and depression. What a great and fun combination, right?!

So I made the decision to write about how life goes when you've got the two together.

Lucky, lucky you.

Buckle in my friends. This is the story of figuring out life when it hands you a whole heap of lemons and you don't have the energy to make lemonade or even reach for the gin. It's a funny story about things that aren't that funny and a coming of age story that came a few years later than expected. It's about mortality, health, the pressures of the modern world, trying to be positive when your heart feels like it's being repeatedly trodden on by an elephant and finding humour in getting diagnosed with breast cancer aged 26 when you carry a black dog around with you every day.

It's essentially about the life of every twenty-something - but with some added mental anguish and the mild inconvenience which is cancer thrown into the mix.

A recipe for disaster? Maybe.

A good story? Hopefully.

A Boobsaurus

THERE ARE SO MANY WORDS FOR BOOBS. I hate repetition when I'm writing, so I made a "boobsaurus" (a thesaurus just including words for boobs) during my treatment for breast cancer. Just saying breasts over and over again would get super dull, super quickly. **And I'm sure there are so, so many more than these. But here's just a few of my faves**

BREASTS
Baps
Basoomas
Bing Bongs
Booballoos
Boobies
Bosoms
Boulders
Breasticles
Breasties
Bristol Cities
Buoyancy aids
Cahoonas
Chebs (personal favourite)
Chesticles
Coconuts
Dairy/Dirty pillows
Disdats
Floaters
Funbags
Honkers
Hooters
Humps
Jugs

Jumper stretchers
Knockers
Lady lumps
Lady mountains
Mary-Kate and Ashleys
Melons
Mosquito bites
Motorboaters
Nips
Norks
Nunga nungas
Pancakes
Passion pouffes
Puppies
Rack
The Twins
Tits
Titties
Titty la la's
Twin airbags
Udders
Wabs
Wibbly wobblies
Ya tats

Chapter 2: The Blues

Before you get ahead of yourself, the "blue" I'm going to be talking about is not the hit 90's classic by Eiffel 65, nor the boy band of "All Rise" fame. I will tell you that I'm probably going to be singing both of those songs to myself while I'm writing this chapter though. They are both absolute bangers after all.

Anyway - on to the matter at hand.

I don't remember when I started to have what I quickly came to describe as "blue days". I don't think I was a particularly anxious child. Perhaps she's just being nice but my Mum always told me that I was the sort of kid that would brighten up a room when they went into it. I was pretty lively. Often laughing, generally pretty well behaved but with a healthy dollop of mischief thrown in.

I had a pretty happy childhood - not without its problems - but it's not like I was dragged up kicking and screaming by the scruff of my neck. I might not have been allowed to have a Tamagotchi or a Furby (that was probably just good sense on my parents' part) but I had everything I needed. My memories of my childhood are largely hugely good. I was happy. I had two parents who loved me and a sister who tormented me in the style one usually expects an older sister to persecute her younger sibling. My sister's treatment may have left me with some unreasonable phobias, but I came out relatively unharmed. Please don't ever try and stick a sticker on me. It will not end well for either of us.

We didn't have a lot of money. I know that there were times we went without certain things but I never noticed. My parents made a lot of sacrifices to protect both my sister and me from a range of financial, relationship and health issues that probably made their lives pretty tough, but I was sheltered from it. My Mum had a difficult childhood, growing up in the underprivileged industrial town of Billingham, near Middlesbrough at a time when education was not a priority and money was not widely seen in the area. She had her own battles - but those stories are not mine to tell.

Home life disregarded as a possible cause for "the blues", I wonder if the years I had at school were more affecting than I realised at the time. I loved my primary school. Between reception and year 6, I was, as my Dad told me many a time, a big fish in a small pond. The teachers knew me, the other students knew me, I knew all of them. That was just the way I liked it. I remember sobbing, feeling as though my heart was about to fall right out of my mouth and onto the table in front of me as I left my Year 6 classroom on that fateful July day in 1999, never to return to the comfort of a school where I could see my Mum in the dining room at lunch time, or where I knew all of the dinner ladies by name, or where I'd end up in my favourite teacher's class again for the fourth year in a row.

Instead, the following September I found myself at Big School. I absolutely hated it.

My secondary school was the type where you were either bullied or you were a bully. There was nothing in between. I was picked on for reading too many books, laughed at for knowing the answers in class, teased for wearing the wrong kind of clothes. Unpleasant, yes, but all very banal things that I can't imagine are responsible for any long-lasting effect on my mental health. I was never subjected to violence, was never shoved aggressively into a prickly hedge, an act often referred to as "heducation", nor did I carry a means of cyberbullying around with me in my coat pocket like kids do today. I struggled through secondary school, but I came out remarkably unscathed. Sometimes I watch programmes like "Educating Yorkshire" and "Educating Essex" and I wonder how any of us got out of secondary school alive. Feeling your way through a social minefield at a time when you don't know what you want to eat for dinner let alone who you are, what you want to do with your life, or who you are going to become feels nigh on impossible. But, for the most part, we all made it through.

So that leads me to suggest that it is simply science that can explain why I am the way I am, perhaps with a dose of genetics thrown in for good measure.

I'm no doctor, but it seems that a simple, chemical imbalance in my brain is to blame for the fact that it sometimes runs down a path to darkness faster than Usain Bolt sprints down a 100m track at the Olympics. That same imbalance is probably to blame for the fact I sometimes find myself worrying for hours on end, or for days, about whether or not I offended that person on the train when I asked them politely if I could please squeeze past them. Did they think I was calling them fat? Did they think I was rude? Aggressive? Pushy? A hipster dick in a stupid blouse and high-waisted jeans?

Similarly, my serotonin-deficient brain is probably responsible for the fact that sometimes I feel suffocated by the news. I know everyone is affected by bad news. When we hear about another shooting in the USA, I know I'm not alone in feeling saddened by the abominable gun laws of the leading country in the world, but it's not uncommon for this kind of news to result in me taking to my bed for three days, strangled by the state of the world we live in, as if I'm some turn of the century damsel who swoons at the slightest hint of misfortune. About 80% of my social media feed is made up of news organisations because of the line of work I'm in - I need to know what's going on to know what I should be writing about, so escaping the bad news often borders on the impossible.

If I'm already on the brink of darkness, it's all too easy for me to be pushed over the edge when I hear a story that particularly affects me.

Science can probably also explain why I still don't always believe that people I consider to be my closest friends and confidantes actually like me and aren't just putting up with me for a reason I simply cannot fathom. Truth be told, even at 13 I was convinced my now best friend couldn't possibly want to spend time with me because why would she when I was a library-dwelling, solo lunch eating dweeb who read too many books*?

*NB - not possible to read too many books

But it took me such a long time to realise that not everyone is like this. While we all have our own idiosyncrasies, our own quirks and foibles, I didn't realise that having days, or weeks where you feel like you're wading through treacle is not a universal thing. I didn't know that other people don't often feel like they can't breathe because the weight of the world is pressing down on them after another horrible news story unfolds in our 24-hours-a-day world of rolling bad news. I couldn't grasp that most people didn't play over the tiniest decisions about something completely inconsequential time and time and time and time again until they made themselves feel physically sick at the thought of whether they said the right thing in that text to their very oldest friend.

I thought everyone felt those things.

I thought everyone knew what it was like to wake up and feel terrified at the prospect of waking up every day for another 70 years.

I thought everyone was afflicted with a voice in their head that offers up negative talk so harsh it borders on being abusive. I thought everyone called themselves "a fucking useless idiot", "waste of space", "dickhead", and says things like "well no-one's going to like you after that you dipshit".

I thought everyone talked to themselves that way.

SPOILER ALERT. I was wrong.

That's not to say I'm alone in this. Far from it in fact. With one in four people in the UK expected to suffer with mental health problems in their lifetimes, there's a lot of people living with issues like, and far worse, than these. And to be honest, I'm not even sure this is the half of what my brain puts me through, but more on that later. It has taken me a long time to unpick the nuances of my thoughts and realise what is me and what is the depression.

For a very long time, I didn't talk to anyone about the fact that my mind and I were essentially engaged in hand-to-hand combat 24 hours a day, seven days a week, 365 days a year. There are still a lot of people in my life who don't know the extent of the depression that I have lived with for most of my adult life.

Eventually, Chris managed to peel back the layers and help me deal with my issues a little bit at a time. He began to recognise when the darkness was closing in and learned to deal with it accordingly. We spoke often about whether or not I should go to the doctors for more professional help, usually when I emerged, blinking and shellshocked from a particularly bad bout of the blues, but we decided time and time again that we could manage it ourselves. Between us, we could keep me on an even keel.

Don't tell him I said this, but I think it takes a very special person to love and support a person with depression, especially untreated and undiagnosed depression, but luckily I found one of them when I was 17.

Note - there are lots of very special people out there. Far more than we remember sometimes - so if you're crushed under a weight of depression and feel like there will never be anyone to love you because of your illness, please know that there will be.

It reached a point though where my depression was becoming more of a hindrance than we knew how to deal with. It was becoming bigger than both of us, perhaps triggered by the aforementioned death of my maternal grandmother. I was at a loss. The periods of darkness were becoming longer and thicker and the holes I was falling into were becoming deeper and more difficult to claw my way out of. I went for days when I didn't feel anything at all. Not sadness, not anger or frustration, just a crushing and debilitating emptiness. I felt hollow and desolate.

But I was paranoid that I wasn't actually depressed. That I was making the whole thing up. I became obsessed with the thought that admitting I had depression meant I was selfish and self-centred and really I just needed to get a bloody grip. Because that's the other great thing about depression - it makes you question literally everything you know about yourself.

I found myself thinking that maybe I was just depressed because I wanted to be? There's always been a stigma around mental health and there definitely still is, but as the internet began to pave the way for people to start tearing that stigma down and more and more people opened up about their own mental health struggles, I wondered if I was just feeling this way because it had become the new "cool" thing to do. I began to worry that any problems I had were first world problems. Irrelevant in the grand scheme of things. Tiny insignificant details that to many would seem as small as if I had just forgotten to ask for marshmallows on my hot chocolate. I constantly ask myself what right do I have to complain about my life when there are people starving, or in war zones, literally fighting every day to find sufficient food to survive or struggling to avoid bombs that drop on their towns and villages. That's ridiculous, right? But these are the sort of tricks your brain plays on you when you suffer with low mood and anxiety.

I suppose the turning point for me, the time when I realised that I was struggling with something very real, when it became apparent that I couldn't cope with this alone, despite the incredible support system my long-term partner had provided me with, was the day I heard the news that Robin Williams had died.

We were in the process of buying a flat (I know - I know how lucky I am to be able to say that, especially in LONDON) and had found ourselves with no fixed address for a month while we waited to complete on the sale. I was flicking through Facebook when I saw it, first thing in the morning. My legs wavered beneath me. I immediately felt sick. I was so affected by the idea that someone as talented and revered as Robin Williams could have reached the very lowest of the low, resulting in him taking his own life. I knew, as much as one can from press reportage, that he was fighting his own black dog, attempting to train it with drugs and alcohol. But what a sad and terrible state of affairs that such a brilliant man was held hostage by his own brain, so much so that he saw no other way out. How unfair that we live in a world where people feel like death is their only option.

We'll never know the reasons for his death, but one thing I do know is that it led to a wide conversation about depression and suicide. Social media was littered with messages from other respected celebrities, calling for their followers to reach out if they needed help. Reminders that they were not alone. Everyone from Russell Brand to Mindy Kaling and Eddie Izzard shared their thoughts on the untimely and cruel demise of one of the brightest stars in my lifetime. People began talking about their own daily arguments with their brain - whether with depression or anxiety, or OCD, or schizophrenia. People began talking about their own darkest thoughts. It became apparent that while Robin Williams may have felt very much alone in the last of his hours, or days, or months, he had reached millions of people through his death.

All of these conversations made me consider the state of my own flawed mental health.

Obviously I did not know Robin Williams, other than through so many of the brilliant films that taught me about comedy in my youth, but I was as haunted by his death as if he had been a family member. It's a number of years since he died but I'm still haunted by it. It sent me into a tailspin of my own darkness. It remains the celebrity death I have been most affected by to date. It became a mirror for my own problems and made me sit up and pay attention to the things happening in my own life.

I admitted to myself that I had depression.

Eventually, I made an appointment to go to the doctors.

Things People Say About Depression:

"Yoga helps with depression"

"Maybe if you just buck up you'll feel better?"

"Have you tried just not being sad?"

"Fresh air is a great cure for depression"

"You shouldn't be taking those antidepressants you know. Antidepressants are a scam"

"Have you got outside recently?"

"It's all about state of mind!"

"You're just not trying hard enough to feel alright"

"Have you thought about going Vegan?"

"But you don't look depressed"

"Stop worrying so much"

"Have you tried pilates?"

"Depression's all in your mind"

"Maybe you should try not thinking about it"

"Think about people who aren't as fortunate as you"

"It could be worse…"

"Have you tried just not being depressed?"

"But think about all the wonderful things in your life!"

"You're stronger than this"

"Just get a hold of yourself!"

"Have you tried drinking more water?"

"You should try smiling more"

"You're so sensitive"

"I saw a programme that said cold water swimming cures depression"

"You're not depressed!"

"Just ignore all these feelings and they'll go away"

"Stop feeling so sorry for yourself"

"I don't believe in depression!"

Things People Would Never Say About Cancer:

"Yoga helps with cancer"

"Maybe if you just buck up you'll feel better?"

"Have you tried just not having cancer?"

"Fresh air is a great cure for cancer"

"You shouldn't be having that chemotherapy you know.
Chemotherapy is a scam"

"Have you got outside recently?"

"It's all about state of mind!"

"You're just not trying hard enough to feel alright"

"Have you thought about going Vegan?"

"But you don't look like you've got cancer"

"Stop having cancer so much"

"Have you tried pilates?"

"Cancer is all in your mind"

"Maybe you should try not thinking about it"

"Think about people who aren't as fortunate as you"

"It could be worse..."

"Have you tried just not having cancer?"

"But think about all the wonderful things in your life!"

"You're stronger than this"

"Just get a hold of yourself!"

"Have you tried drinking more water?"

"You should try smiling more"

"You're so sensitive"

"I saw a programme that said cold water swimming cures
cancer"

"You don't have cancer!"

"Just ignore the cancer and it'll go away!"

"Stop feeling so sorry for yourself"

"I don't believe in cancer!"

Chapter 3: Doctors and Depression

It doesn't matter how many times you read that talking is the first step to improving your mental health, actually taking steps to begin these conversations is often painful and distressing for those who really need to talk. With the NHS in its current condition, there are people across the country who are repeatedly asking for help but not getting anywhere. If you are in a position where you can get an appointment with your GP, there's nothing more exposing than sitting in front of that medical professional and saying "Hi. Hello. Yes. I need help because my brain and I aren't quite on the same page at the moment and it's proving a little bit problematic". Or than finding yourself in front of a complete stranger in floods of tears after they ask you the (seemingly totally innocuous question) "what can I do for you today?"

I recently talked at a festival (Trew Fields - the UK's first holistic health and cancer awareness festival, brainchild of my phenomenal friend Sophie Trew and her partner in crime Will Herman) about my experiences of mental health and was asked why there's such a stigma around mental health - not just from Joe Public and the media, but from the person experiencing mental health problems themselves. I had never really considered that I was guilty of stigmatising myself - but I absolutely was. And it's something I continue to do, despite having garnered some kind of handle on my mental health situation. The dictionary definition of to "stigmatise" is to "describe or regard as worthy of disgrace or great disapproval". When you consider that the crux of depression and anxiety often comes down to self-worth and self-belief, it's really no wonder those who engage in protracted battles with their inner dialogue find themselves frustrated, angry and disappointed with their own propensity to overthink.

Every time I considered talking to a medical professional, I felt like a fraud. I worried they'd laugh me out of the building, shouting frantically after me "LOL how can you, a white, middle class cisgender woman have depression? You've got it so good lady, you don't even know what depression is! You're a fool if you think you have anything to be depressed about!" I catastrophised even the possibility of an appointment so badly - exploring every single thing a GP could say to me that would prove that I was a failure, an idiot and an attention seeker who was making up that they'd thought about stepping out in front of a train - that actually making an appointment was tantamount to climbing Mount Everest. I pictured every scenario under the sun where I'd leave my surgery feeling more like an idiot than when I'd arrived.

There was absolutely no reason for me to feel this way. Chris has worked with GPs for years and I've never met a single one of his colleagues who gave me any indication that they wouldn't take seriously someone who feels depressed if they cropped up in their clinic. The GPs I know as a result of Chris' career and in my own circles are nothing but a wonderful, kind, considerate and thoughtful bunch who take pride in their jobs and work their absolute backsides off to do the best for their patients. It doesn't matter how hard they are working, how busy they are, what kind of politics is unfolding behind the scenes, I do not know a single GP who wouldn't take the time to work with someone who was experiencing a mental health crisis. So why did I think my GP would treat me any differently? Because I was stigmatising myself into thinking that I wasn't deserving of their empathy.

Despite my continual efforts of self-sabotage and stigmatisation, eventually I managed to make an appointment and force myself to go. Unsurprisingly, the GP I visited offered the perfect example of how to treat someone who was struggling with their mental health. She listened attentively, took the time to ask me questions, handed me tissues when I became an uncontrollable puddle of snot and tears. She didn't laugh at me. She didn't suggest I was being ridiculous. She didn't tell me that my life was too good for me to be susceptible to becoming depressed. She didn't judge me. She told me I was brave for taking a step to come and see her. She told me that I deserved better than not being able to get out of bed when I felt too empty to even consider existing. She told me I deserved to be well and happy. And I believed her. For the first time in a long time, I believed that I deserved more than my current existence. She talked to me about my options - from counselling and cognitive behavioural therapy (CBT) and other talking therapies to considering medication. I told her I was reticent to begin taking tablets but I was happy to try some talking therapies.

But the way the NHS was at the time meant that I needed more than just an understanding doctor to start getting treatment. Having found myself in the warmth of her understanding, she told me I needed to fill out a self referral form for the local Improving Access to Psychological Therapies (IAPT) service. The process of self-referring refuelled all the frantic thoughts I'd had before the appointment. I took the form and sat in the doctor's surgery waiting room while I tried to quantify my depression by gauging how many times I had been depressed in the last 14 days. I clutched desperately to the piece of paper that could offer me a solution to my ongoing issues but was paralysed by the fear that my answers to the questions would show I was making a big deal about nothing. I worried I wouldn't be considered "depressed enough" and the opportunity for wellness would be taken away from me when I was revealed as a fraud who should have been able to get on with things like everyone else did. Looking back now, I see that these concerns show just how much I was in my head, just how much I was feeding myself lies and putting myself down. These patterns show just how depressed I was and just how desperate I was for help. I filled out the form, left the surgery and cried.

Unlike with cancer, I was never explicitly told that I did, as I suspected, have a combination of depression and anxiety. They didn't say the words because there's no definitive test to say whether you do or whether you don't. The forms you fill out (where you mark how you've felt on a sliding scale and the totals add up to give an indication of your mental state) and the things you say give an indication but in reality, the only person who can know the severity of your symptoms is you. The first GP I saw told me it certainly seemed like I needed some support, counselling and I would benefit from medication. It's funny because if I think about the moment I was diagnosed with cancer and the moment I was "diagnosed" with depression, the two experiences are totally different. I think this plays a huge part in the differentiation in perception and treatment of mental vs physical symptoms: mental symptoms are so much harder to wrap your hands (or minds) around and as such are harder to diagnose and in turn, harder to understand. If you present at the hospital with a broken leg, an x-ray, a *scientific* test which cannot be argued with, will demonstrate that your tibia has a crack the size of a needle in it. When you go to a GP and tell them that you feel like your brain is on fire as a result of endless and aggressive negative thoughts, there is no scientific test which cannot be disputed. People can't see mental distress in the same way they can see a broken bone. So the two are never conflated as part of the same puzzle. But they really, truly are.

***

Waiting times for treatment for mental health services are something which is talked and written about at length. In 2017, I wrote a piece for Stylist titled "How to look after yourself while waiting for NHS mental health support" and explained:

"It's widespread knowledge that one in four people in the UK will engage in some sort of battle with their brain at least once during their lifetime. From anxiety to depression, and everything in between, the mind is a difficult beast to tame – and it seems society is finally becoming more accepting of this as a common truth. More people than ever are turning to the NHS for support: in fact, **1.4 million people** were referred for talking therapies in 2015 and 2016.

However, there is no denying that the NHS is stretched. Mental health services are woefully underfunded and it's taking time for people to access the help that they've so bravely sought out. The NHS aims to see those who have been referred for psychiatric support for mild to moderate issues within a maximum of 18 weeks, in line with wait times for physical health issues, and **88% of people are currently seen within this timeframe. But waiting over four months, having taken the steps to seek help from a GP, can be painstaking at such a crucial time.**"

If my memory serves me (which to be honest, in this life post-chemo, I can't guarantee), I had a call from IAPT to ascertain my needs within about a month of visiting my GP. As I sat in a graveyard near my office, one of the only quiet places near the bustling business district I worked in in London, trying my hardest to appear together and collected when all I wanted to do was cry, I was told that the information I'd shared with them on my referral form and the way I talked about my mental health suggested that I definitely qualified and would benefit from some guidance. I was put on the list for CBT and told I'd have an appointment in four to six weeks. I was so ashamed. I was ashamed that I couldn't help myself and had been forced to seek an intervention from medical professionals. I told barely anyone about that call and as soon as I hung up the phone, I slipped straight back into that self-stigmatisation.

I always say that when you're seeking guidance for the trickier aspects of your brain, things often get worse before they get better. I say that because that's what I know from my personal experience. After that call, things began to unravel for me at a dramatic pace. If I'd been struggling before, I was certainly struggling in the wake of actually admitting I needed help and waiting for it. The depressed side of my brain, the one which told me I was an idiot and a fool and a liar and useless was engaged in a fairly consistent hand-to-hand combat battle with the side of my brain that was starting to realise what was going on in there wasn't quite as it should be. And of the two voices, the negative one was much louder, much more persistent and much more boisterous (as is always the way).

Between my call with IAPT and my first appointment, I had talked myself into so many knots I resembled a cat's cradle in the levels it's almost impossible to navigate your way out of. I had convinced myself it was a terrible idea and a waste of time. I had convinced myself that actually, if I had to accept any form of help, I just needed to talk, rather than come up with "strategies" to help me avoid taking an emotional nosedive when the Dark Place tried to tempt me into it. Because that's what CBT aims to do. According to the NHS:

"CBT is a talking therapy that can help you manage your problems by changing the way you think and behave. CBT is based on the concept that your thoughts, feelings, physical sensations and actions are interconnected, and that negative thoughts and feelings can trap you in a vicious cycle. CBT aims to help you deal with overwhelming problems in a more positive way by breaking them down into smaller parts. You're shown how to change these negative patterns to improve the way you feel."

Generally, I'm a pretty open minded person, but this all felt so abstract to me. I couldn't fathom how it might help me break the long-established patterns of self-doubt, self-criticism, self-loathing and generally poor mental health I was living in the middle of. These were things that I had embedded in my mindset over a lifetime and it was almost impossible to even consider how a few techniques taught to me by a total stranger would help me fill in the long-standing trenches these thought patterns had created in the depths of my brain and my soul. I was a shell of a person who felt like there was no way to navigate my way out of these habits. As it happened, my CBT counsellor became a hand that yanked me from those trenches and helped me begin filling them in. I know it seems unlikely but talking about myself has never been something that comes easily to me. All too often I am self-deprecating - I make jokes about my idiosyncrasies and present myself as a bit of a clown in an attempt to bury the shell of my darkness deep down inside. But at CBT I was immediately plunged into a position where, to get the most out of my experience, I had to give in to exposing the parts of my brain I'd never shared with anyone before. CBT became a mirror I couldn't avoid. Talking about and exploring the thoughts that plagued me during my depressive episodes made me feel sick. Every time I relived the thought processes that had dominated my life for such a long time and unpicked them with my CBT counsellor shockwaves were sent through my body.

Every session felt like an hour of catching my funny-bone on a sharp edge (is it just me or does that feeling genuinely get more intense as you get older?). But we made progress. Slowly but surely, we unpacked and unpicked the things that triggered my periods of low mood. My therapist taught me how to recognise the thoughts I'd always accepted as normal for the damaging and restricting things they really were. I began to realise how much what was going on in my head had impacted and affected every aspect of my life. I'll never forget the day my therapist told me that most of the things I was telling myself on the regular were thoughts not facts*. He made me consider how every thought I had would stand if I were in front of a jury. In a court of law, thoughts are irrelevant. They deal in facts alone. And most of the things I told myself were true ("you're useless", "you're fat", "everyone hates you", "you're worthless", "you don't deserve to be happy" - even to "you're making all of this up because you're an attention seeking maggot") had no evidentiary proof to back them up. So why did I believe all of the things I said to myself for so long?

The revelation that I was telling myself lies and I didn't have to take my thoughts as read was a massive lifeshock* for me. It offered endless opportunities to open myself to change and evolution, a process I'm still working on every day.

As my CBT sessions continued, it became apparent that my mental health issues stemmed from dramatically low self-esteem. Over time, I discovered patterns and began to unravel the pre-conditioning I had developed that made me react the way I did.

*Incidentally, without wanting to go off piste too much, this is what writer and speaker Sophie Sabbage would call a "lifeshock" moment which she describes as thus: "*Lifeshock.* Noun. *An unwanted or unexpected moment in time, offering an opportunity for personal awakening.*"

These patterns weren't easy to begin to break through. They were based on a lifetime (albeit a fairly short one, but a lifetime nonetheless) of habits. A study of 96 people published in *The European Journal of Social Psychology* explains that a habit takes 66 days to form and 21 days to break.

But when those habits have become engrained over 10,000 days or thereabouts, as mine had, reframing this kind of behaviour is a much more stretched out project than it would be to add a piece of fruit into your daily elevenses. That's not to say you can't start to see change in those 21 days, but when thought patterns and processes are embedded into every crevice of your brain and reflect out into your daily life, it's hard to recognise them for what they are and react accordingly. To be honest, a lot of the things I learned in the CBT sessions I had before cancer is lost on me now. It's like my brain had to make way for all of the new information it was taking in after getting my diagnosis and all of the stuff I had learned fell out of my ear or something. Interestingly enough, the song lyrics from 90's "hit" Mr Smurftastic are still deeply embedded in my consciousness, but most of what I had learned in CBT evaporated. I hadn't had the chance to give the techniques I had been learning time to stick before my whole world was turned upside-down and shaken around like a snow globe.

But there are two things that have stuck with me and I continue to carry with me as much as I can. If you know me in real life, you might be aware of a little tattoo I have on my left forearm of three triangles, the top one of which is shaded in. I always think it's a bit rude when people ask "but what does that *mean*?" about tattoos because they're so personal and I feel a bit awkward when I'm put on the spot but to me, this is a daily reminder of something I gleaned from that six session course of CBT. It means "thoughts not facts". It's a reminder that everything I tell myself should be assessed and examined to establish whether I have evidentiary proof that it is a fact, or whether it's a thought - something unsubstantiated I am telling myself. It reminds me to explore the things I hear from myself and examine their veracity. I know this sounds like a pretty arduous process, and it can be. It just gives me a chance to break, to breathe and figure out which parts of my daily dialogue with myself are true. And that breath in itself is a blessing. If you have a tendency to let your thoughts run away with you a bit too, taking a pause to have these conversations with yourself is completely invaluable. It can stop you chasing an ardently negative thought in the same way an enthusiastic child would run down the street after an ice-cream van. Although, let's be fair, pretty much every adult I know wants to run down the street after an ice-cream van every time they hear its dulcet tones too. That's slightly off topic and nullifies my metaphor. But you get the point.

"Thoughts not Facts" is one of the longstanding CBT techniques I try to bring into my everyday. I don't manage to assess the truth of every single thought I have, but the big ones, the real kick-you-when-you're-down, stomp-on-your-gut-and-tell-you-you're-a-failure thoughts can be easier to tentatively discard when you've put them through this process. Ask yourself the questions Steve used to ask me - would what you're telling yourself stand up in a court of law? Could it be used as proof in a criminal case? Is this backed up by evidence? And more often than not with the horrid things we tell ourselves, the answer is no.

Along with all the other things I tell myself, one of the often recurring thoughts I have, as I mentioned before, is that I'm making this whole thing up. That I'm just experiencing the same as everyone else but I'm not tough enough to take it. My serotonin deficient brain often tries to convince me that my thoughts and feelings are invalid which is a vicious cycle, and one I was told by a psychotherapist was indicative of just how deep my depression runs.

I've been on the receiving end of the statement "you're the most positive person I know!" more times than I'd care to remember, especially in light of my cancer diagnosis and at times I am positive. My disposition is naturally fairly sunny but when the dark clouds roll over, I strap a smile on my face until I can crawl through the front door at home, crumble into a heap and sleep for 24 hours. There's only one person who sees this version of me. A few of my closest friends and family had an inkling that that person existed, but most of the people I know had no idea 'till I wrote a blog post called Confession Time and shoehorned in a reference to the Foo Fighters back in November 2016, just after the idea for this book had come about. So it's all too easy for me to tell myself that if so many people I know see a happy-go-lucky-smiling-faced-dreamer in me but I can't see it in myself, it must be me that's wrong. Not them. 'Cos they all know me better than I know myself, amirite?

Look, I know how ridiculous this is. But this is genuinely what it's like to live with a mind like mine and I know that there are so many others in the world who will recognise these feelings and thoughts as their own. Self-doubt doesn't impact my perception of my abilities, but it goes into the very core of my being. I doubt that I can be loved (even when I know, *like really, truly* know that is not the case), I distrust my judgement, my decision making, my relationships. I don't trust the universe when it throws opportunities my way. I question my worth and my value.

So when I say I am depressed, I don't mean I'm just sad. That's not to say I don't get sad in the standard sense. I absolutely do. My mental health botherations don't stop me from feeling all the emotions any other human feels sometimes. I can be in a state of sadness without being in the crux of a depressive episode. I can feel desolate and see that there is a way out of that feeling. But when I'm in the clutches of a particularly bad bout of low mood, these things are either all the more intense, or completely numbed by a blanket of nothingness. When anyone with depression says they are depressed, they mean they're having this sort of multi-faceted, all encompassing dispute with themselves. It's no wonder people with clinical depression are exhausted all the time. I feel tired just writing about this stuff, let alone feeling it all and trying to quiet the louder voice with one that's kinder and more reassuring. That process of fact-checking every thought I mentioned earlier takes time and energy.

The thing is though, every person's experience of depression and mental health problems is different. It may be that their depression is exacerbated by crippling anxiety or perhaps they experience periods of mania in among the periods of low mood. Depression can be linked to hormones, it can be triggered by experiences. Often there's no real causality for it. I recently listened to an episode of Bryony Gordon's podcast *Mad World* featuring the incredible Stephen Fry who commented "if you can explain why you're sad, it's not really depression". And it's so true. So very, very true. The sadness of depression is inexplicable. And it's so much more than sadness.

Despite the similarities in thought processes, no two people's experience will be the same. It's cliched but I often think of that quote that says "You never know what someone is going through. Be kind. Always". Even those with the same "condition" have different experiences. And I know that for those who don't have experience of mental health problems it can seem impossible to navigate other people's tumultuous brain processes but, as with most things in life, kindness is key. If you know someone who has depression, being kind is often enough. Because if you can guarantee one thing, it's that in their darkest moments, they're not being kind to themselves.

Notes from a Mixed Up Mind

- A friend sends me a draft of their wedding Save the Date to ask what it looks like. I can't decipher the pun and I worry that I have let them down for about 30 mins

- I worry that when mentioning my upcoming holiday to a business acquaintance they think I'm bragging. Reminded of this every time I speak to them for a few weeks

- I watch a programme about our country's reliance on drugs. I know my antidepressants make my life better. I know that, for me, they are a lifesaver. I worry whether I should come off them. Am I weak for taking antidepressants? Should I be better than I am?

- I haven't had a dark day in a while. I begin to worry about when it will come. I begin to wonder whether I ever really had depression, or whether I've made the whole thing up

- I worry that getting diagnosed with cancer at 26 means my card has been marked, and I'm meant to die. I've defied death by beating cancer, so surely it's just a matter of time 'til death catches up with me

- Someone I've been working with keeps calling me Alice-May. When I meet them, I worry they're going to think I was rude for not telling them they could just call me ALICE. The reason I didn't tell them they could just call me ALICE before meeting them is because I worried they would think I was being rude

- I worry I am swallowing too loudly while I'm having a massage. Should I have shaved my legs before I came to this appointment? Does my therapist think I have disgusting feet? God they must really hate touching me

- I worry I am talking about cancer too much when I'm almost two years out of treatment

- Why aren't I running the London Marathon, only three weeks after finishing treatment for breast cancer? All of these people are managing to do it

- No-one wants to read this piece of shit you're writing. Why do you think they do? What authority do you think you have on this subject?

- I worry that three days after major surgery, I'm not fatigued or dealing with the effects of an anaesthetic and healing from the trauma that being operated on is, but I'm just really lazy

- I deserve to die. Why else did I get cancer?

- Maybe I am not depressed. Maybe I am a pathological liar who just wants attention

- No-one would miss me if I wasn't here

- I don't know how to survive in a world post-cancer

- I booked my doctors appointment for 11.30am. But maybe the appointment is at 10.10am and I'm going to be late

- What if my neighbours can hear what I'm watching on Netflix and are judging me for watching another episode of Gilmore Girls?

- I just sniffed once on the tube. Everyone hates me

- We get back from holiday and I spend 85% of the journey home worrying that there has been a flood, or the flat has burnt down, or that there are dead mice in the sink

- I'm talking too much. I'm talking about myself too much. Everyone will think I'm selfish and narcissistic

- I am irrationally worried that I have not achieved anything with my life *(this one is pretty constant).* I am a useless member of society and I am letting everyone down. I am a drain on the NHS and I do not provide society with anything of benefit

- I worry that I am terrible at therapy and my therapist hates me. I worry she thinks I'm a loser who needs to get a grip

- I have a conversation with my therapist in which she suggests I won't have depression forever. I ask her if that means I made the whole thing up in the first place.

- Maybe I should be able to just "snap out of it"

- My computer feels a bit warm. I worry it's going to explode

- Sometimes I think I deserve to get secondary breast cancer. And I don't argue with myself because living in a world until I am 90 years old terrifies me. And dying from cancer would be a way out

- I worry that by thinking that, I'm letting everyone down. That I'm a terrible person and it's disrespectful to everyone who has died because of this disease

- I have a consistent pain in my collarbone that lasts for weeks and weeks. I tell myself I am wasting everyone's time, energy and the

NHS' money by getting it checked out.

- I am letting cancer define me and that is a bad thing. Letting cancer define me means I am failing to be a good survivor

- I am not worthy of feeding and hydrating

- My ideas are useless. I can't write anything. I will never amount to anything

- I worry that my husband will hate my cooking (he has never had a bad thing to say about anything I have ever cooked before)

- Everyone thinks I'm a boring waste of space who just bangs on ALL THE TIME about that one time I had cancer

- Go to vote in local elections. Spend quite a long time worrying I accidentally voted Conservative instead of Labour. For months after the Brexit referendum, I worry I accidentally voted to leave the EU, rather than remain (I DEFINITELY DID NEITHER OF THESE THINGS I PROMISE)

- I worry that everyone will think the things on this list are stupid

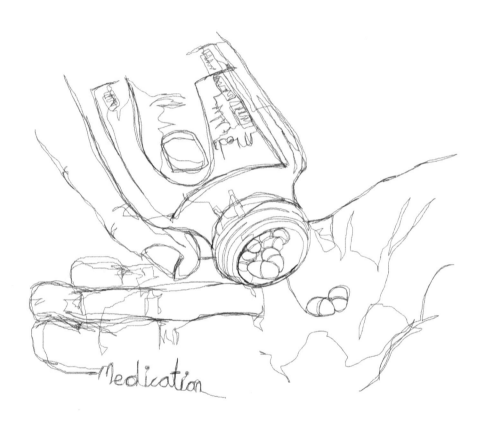

Medication

Chapter 4: Medication

When I was a kid, I struggled a bit with asthma. It seems that if there's a weak spot in the historic health of my family, it's our ability to breathe well under duress. Any one of us in the Purkiss clan who gets a cold ends up with a hacking cough - you know, the sort that people move away from on the bus. The sort that makes people glare at you on the tube. Or one that once upon a time earned me the filthiest looks I have ever received when I had the audacity to have a chest infection while attending an event at the Royal Albert Hall. When I was a kid, I was given inhalers to deal with my problem. I dutifully took my brown inhaler every day to prevent the symptoms. I took the blue inhaler when I needed instant relief, or when I wanted to look like I needed to stop running in cross country, which, truth be told, was often.

At age 13, I had horrible problems with my periods. They were heavy, full of clots, and often left me completely washed out, a weird white-grey colour and regularly unable to hold my head upright. I went to the doctors. I was given tablets. I tried these tablets. They didn't work. I tried other tablets. They didn't work. Eventually I was put on the pill. Every day, I took this little tablet to try to control my periods. I stayed on the pill for about ten years and the problematic periods faded to being pretty manageable. Well, as manageable as periods can be, given that a large portion of the population finds them utterly hellish. But the medication helped.

There was a time when I regularly got migraines so severe that the right hand side of my face would droop. I actually looked a bit like I'd had a stroke. It took a while for these migraines to bugger off, with my symptoms often lasting for four or five days. I saw a neurologist who put me on a preventative tablet. I took this every day to "break the cycle" of the migraines, which were clearly linked to my menstrual cycle (sorry for mentioning periods twice in two paragraphs, but some people bleed out of their uteruses, uteri?, around once every 28 days and I have been one of them, soooo, buck up Bronco). I was on these tablets for over a year, no questions asked.

So why is it then, when a doctor suggested to me that I went on medication to combat the crippling depression I was experiencing, I resisted? Why did I think that my brain not working quite as I would have liked it to was any different to my lungs not working quite as I'd like them to? While not quite as useful an excuse to skive out of PE (perhaps that's a discussion for another time?), it was still a problem for me. By this point my depression had begun pervading my life in a noticeable way - forcing me to confront the issue head on and go to the GP for support. If it had once been a cloud lingering over my shoulder, it was now a surrounding fog that refused to budge. I was struggling to make even the simplest of decisions on a daily basis. If I managed to drag myself out of bed, get dressed and leave the house, the question of which shoes to wear for a day in the office often left me crippled on the doorstep. Deciding what to have for lunch became such an ordeal it was all too easy to skip lunches. I had begun to feel completely numb and consistently felt as though something awful were about to happen. I lived in a state of anticipating impending doom, a disgusting and suffocating case of "low mood" and a paralysing anxiety. But still, I felt that taking a tablet to help was a foolish step. I think part of me saw it as an admission of weakness, of defeat. I felt like I should be able to handle everything the rest of the world was handling. When a GP pointed out to me that if I was a diabetic, I wouldn't turn down insulin, I realised that perhaps I had been affected by external perspectives on what taking antidepressants means.

It's interesting, isn't it? Because more and more people are talking about their mental health on the regular these days. Thanks to the internet, the conversation has opened up and continues to do so exponentially. As a result, the stigma surrounding discussions of a sensitive nature seems to be fading. But from where I'm sitting, this stigma has relocated. Most people no longer judge others quite so harshly for having issues with their mental health (I'm not arguing that this has completely gone - we've a long way to go on that score) but society is distinctly less forgiving of those who take antidepressants, god forbid they should need to do so over a long period of time. I'm writing this in 2018, but sensationalist headlines like "A Nation Hooked on Happy Pills" are still splashed across the front page of one of the biggest selling newspapers in the country, while previously disgraced journalist Johann Hari has just released a book which begins by throwing doubt on the efficacy of antidepressants. While I've no doubt that Hari genuinely believes the claims in his book it's my firm belief that claims such as these are seriously damaging to huge numbers of people. I *wish* my antidepressants were happy pills that made me as perpetually jolly as the characteristically named Green Giant but they aren't. They help me to be functional some of the time rather than just a shell of a person all of the time. They don't stop me from arriving at The Dark Place, but they do usually mean my stays there aren't as long-lasting or as terrifying. They mean I can usually find my way out of that shit hole. They're the map that means I still have to find my own way, but they are also a light in the dark that helps me figure out what I need to do to escape.

I know that medication doesn't work for everyone, but I also know what a massive difference a small dose of a tablet makes to my life - and the lives of people I love and care about - on a daily basis. As a result, I'm able to recognise the impact of the kind of blasé statement that lambasts people for taking potentially lifesaving drugs. There will be people who read things like this and think they're doing something wrong when they take their little tablet every night after they've brushed their teeth. Even though I absolutely believe that taking drugs like this is right for me, there are times when reading a scathing headline or a review of a book which suggests "everything I know about depression is wrong" will make my resolution falter. If I am in a bad way, I can doubt my decision to take Citalopram every single day. I wonder if I'm making a terrible mistake and come dangerously close to convincing myself to come off them. And I am resolute in my belief that this medication makes my life better. So what about those people for whom medication feels like accepting failure? Or those whose lives are being saved by medication but they feel shamed because they need support from a tablet? This rhetoric puts people like this at genuine risk.

There's a reason the National Union of Journalists bans this kind of colloquialism in reporting - because it is dangerous. Would you ever see a headline that says "A Nation Hooked on Chemotherapy"? No, you would not. Come to think of it, ever seen a colloquialism for chemotherapy used in the press? No. Because people who have chemotherapy are not demonised by the rags who run these types of headlines about mental health problems.

That's not to say that choosing to take medication has been a fix-all for me, or that it was an easy process to begin. I felt like hell on earth for the first two weeks on my "happy pills". It was a while ago now and I've had chemotherapy since then so my memory is a bit mushy but I vividly remember feeling like the whole world was falling down around me in those early days. There was a day when Chris wouldn't leave the house because I had woken up crying and couldn't stop. At the time, I thought he just felt bad leaving me because I was in such a state, but I know now that he felt like he couldn't leave because he wasn't sure if I was a danger to myself. I have no idea if I was a danger to myself but I felt like my chest had been ripped open and I didn't know how to stem the intense emotion that was bleeding out of it. When I wasn't crying, I was lethargic, confused and numb. Without a doubt, the antidepressants initially worsened my symptoms before they made them better. But I was lucky. I had a long-suffering partner who was able to support me as I found my feet and I was well cared for by a stretched but determined primary care system where I had appointments every two weeks in the early days, and every month thereafter until I had settled into the medication. And I'd made the decision to combine my medication with talking therapies, as the two working together in a double pronged approach are believed to be much more beneficial than just opting to stab at depression with a one pronged implement, like a chopstick.

Much like medication, CBT doesn't work for everyone, but I was so lucky that I was able to go and see a practitioner in the flesh so we could not just talk about strategies for keeping depression and anxiety at bay, but to discuss the things that were on my mind. The human interaction of my CBT was hugely beneficial to me. My therapist never made me feel like I was an inconvenience or a fraud or I was wasting his time - all things I had convinced myself he would. And as I moved through the process and learned more techniques and got used to the medication I was on, I slowly started to feel more human. I was finally figuring out who I was with depression and how I could deal with it so it didn't impact my life too much. I had begun to recognise the signals, my triggers, the little notes I left myself to suggest that a dark wave was on its way. But then, to paraphrase Joan Didion, life changes in an instant.

It was just as I was finishing my CBT that I found out I had breast cancer. In fact, I went along to my final CBT session a few days after I'd been told. At the start of every session, I'd sit down with my therapist and he'd ask me that open-ended question "How are you?". And his asking of this question was not the perfunctory greeting we so often offer up to those we meet. It was more loaded, a "how *are* you - really? How is your brain? How is your mood? Have you thought about killing yourself this week? Have you thought about hurting yourself this week? Have you felt at risk at all this week?"

And for the first time, I didn't answer him with a breakdown of what had affected my mood or exacerbated my depression that week. We didn't break down, day by day, things that may have triggered a feeling of lowness. I told him what had happened earlier that week.

"Well, Steve, I've just been diagnosed with breast cancer."

That was not what he was expecting to hear, but then again, neither was it what I was expecting I was going to need to say.

From there, it became a whole other ball game. I dread to think what kind of position I would have found myself in after hearing the words "you have" and "cancer" in the same sentence and relating to me if I hadn't already been seeking help for my volatile mental health. If I hadn't had that CBT and if I hadn't already been on those antidepressants, I genuinely believe that my depression at that moment would have been a bigger threat to my existence than the cancerous tumour growing within my breast.

What was going on in my brain quickly began playing second fiddle to the things I needed to do to prevent the cancer from getting any worse. I quickly slipped into cancer mode and everything I learned about maintaining my own mental health fell into a massive ditch at the side of the treatment road I was hurtling down at alarming speed. I no longer had time to think about the shitty things my brain was telling me, because it was full up with cancer-related thoughts. Was I going to die? Was the cancer going to spread? Should I have a mastectomy? Can they take both my breasts off? Am I a carrier of the BRCA gene? What will that mean for my family if I am? Am I going to die and leave Chris on his own? How will chemotherapy make me feel? What is going to happen?

After being told I had cancer, everything I'd learned in CBT evaporated. It was no longer a priority. My focus swiftly shifted to surviving the cancer. The self-care of checking my thoughts and their patterns felt superfluous when I had something actively trying to kill me growing in my body. For a while there I didn't give my brain anywhere near enough of the attention it needed, when it probably needed it most. I went from combining talking therapies with medication to relying solely on my medication to keep my brain in check. About half way through treatment I found myself really struggling. Christmas 2015 saw me undergo my fourth chemotherapy session. I was exhausted in a way I can't even begin to explain to you. My spirit was broken and I felt like I was losing myself. It was during this period that I hit below rock bottom. I hit sub-zero. I got so low, I could practically feel the heat of the earth's core licking at my feet. I had, as I think most cancer patients do at one point or another, been questioning whether the treatment I was undergoing was worth it. I wondered if it was worth losing my breast and losing my hair and feeling like hell and being poisoned. But for me, there was something else too. I had gradually gained a grip on my depression as I worked through my CBT and cancer had made me forget what I had to do to stay alive, what I had to do to make sure my negative thoughts didn't consume me, didn't take over my life and begin to dominate my waking thoughts. It's something that I hate thinking about now, but at the time I remember wondering, not only was it all worth it, but did I really want to live in a world after cancer? On more than one occasion I have thought to myself, "If only I had left that lump for longer. If only I hadn't been in the habit of checking myself, then perhaps it would have spread, and perhaps I wouldn't be forced to deal with the complex aftermath of surviving this disease". I hate that I thought that. I hate that there are still times when I think about it. Because I have wanted to die in the past, and now, post-cancer there is a reason why I might. Sometimes now, I don't think about killing myself, I think about cancer coming back and doing the job for me.

But my medication was a salvation to me throughout all of this. And it continues to be. It means that those thoughts don't linger as long as perhaps they would have done had I not been medicated. They mean that I don't follow through when my brain is telling me I am worthless and that I do not deserve to be alive. That tiny tablet means the voice - that tells me I should have been the one to die, rather than all the others I know who have had secondary breast cancer diagnoses and who have died as a result of this disease - doesn't shout as loud or is easier to shrug off than it would be without the medication.

And I know I am lucky. I spend my entire life qualifying everything I say about my cancer experience with "I am grateful to still be here," and the truth is, I might be, but sometimes my brain isn't. Sometimes the cruel thoughts in my head tell me that I deserved to get cancer, that I deserved to die from it. That I still deserve to die from it. And it is only a matter of time before I do. And it is a process. It's something that I am constantly working on rectifying.

As I sit here now, overlooking the stunning bay at Port de Soller in Mallorca, watching the birds swoop over the crystalline sea, hearing the bustle of the streets below, wrapped in a blanket and writing about my experience, I am grateful. But I also know that it won't be long until the dogs start snapping at my heels with their messages of self-destruction. And I think this is something that doesn't get spoken about often enough, both in the world at large, and in the world post-cancer.

Citalopram has been a saviour for me. It doesn't come without side effects. I'm heavier than I feel like I should be. I get a dry, metallic taste in my mouth if I don't drink regularly. Perhaps it exacerbates the fatigue that I experience post-cancer. But when the darkness seeps in at the edges of my life, like a blot of watercolour paint on a piece of parchment, spreading slowly across the page, Citalopram slows the progress. It makes the black less dense as it makes its way across my life. It doesn't make the hole I am teetering on the edge of less deep or consuming or terrifying, but it makes it easier to escape from. Citalopram offers a rope to climb. It's still a difficult journey that takes every ounce of strength and leaves my body and mind exhausted from the intense effort, but it makes it doable. It makes getting out of The Dark Place possible.

And I know there are people that say the longer I stay on medication the more likely it is to stop working. I know others argue that it has a placebo effect, that it doesn't actually make any difference. Some believe that I will never be able to come off my tablets, but after the last three years and knowing my own mind as I do, I'm not sure I'd be comfortable coming off them anyway. I have fought long and hard to get to some semblance of "normality" and I still have a long way to go - so why would I give up one thing that makes it easier? I go back to the diabetes reference - I wouldn't give up Insulin just because the newspaper said my "dependence" on it was problematic. I wouldn't turn down the chemotherapy that would save my life. So why are antidepressants any different?

Living through cancer is a nightmare, in so many ways. I'm not saying that every person who experiences a cancer diagnosis needs a prescription for antidepressants, but what I am saying is as simple as this: we need to give our brains the same amount of attention we give our bodies when we are going through cancer treatment. We need talking therapies to deal with what is happening to us. We need counsellors to guide us through the hellfire and treat the internal burns that we get as a result. There is no part of your life that is unaffected by a cancer diagnosis and there is no shame in asking for a hand to grab onto at the scariest time of your life. If you're going through treatment and you are struggling, ask for help. Talk to your medical team about counselling. They know that there is a disconnect between the physical and the mental treatment of cancer and there are conscious efforts being made to bridge that gap. So ask for help. You are not weak, you are not overly emotional, you are not letting the side down by not being positive all the time. You are asking for what you need and that is something to be celebrated.

My friend Sophie Trew is a big believer in the body and brain connection. While this is also an Xbox 360 game apparently, Sophie began learning about the body and brain connection relating to humans, not computer games, after her own diagnosis of blood cancer when she was 23. She created her own holistic wellness plan to run alongside her cancer treatment, focusing on breathwork, meditation, movement and much more. While she may not be shouting about how positivity can heal cancer, she's an advocate for the idea that taking care of your mind can help you take care of your body too. Because the two are inextricably linked.

Whatever you believe about how the brain and the body work together, it's important to remember that some people need more of a helping hand to get their brains on an even keel - and that's OK. Remember, despite what the tabloids might say, if you and your doctor believe you should be on medication to deal with your mental health, cancer diagnosis or no, there is no shame. That's a decision between you and your medical team. Ignore the people who don't know what it's like to live with a gremlin in their heads. Ignore the splashy, attention-grabbing headlines. Ignore the people who bash others down on Twitter. You know your brain better than anyone else. So trust yourself. Even if the gremlin and the media are telling you differently.

How To Look After Yourself when You're Approaching The Dark Place

I'm not going to sit here and tell you that these things will immediately make everything better if you're struggling with your mental health, but this is a list of some of the things that work well for me (and some other people who have written/spoken about their mental health) if I'm teetering close to The Dark Place and I'm far enough away to recognise it. I think a big part of learning to live with depression and anxiety is learning your own healthy coping mechanisms and recognising the things that might be more of a hindrance than a help to your mental welfare. Also, I'm not an expert, but I have a lot of personal experience figuring out what has worked for me and what doesn't - so take some time to figure out what on this list works for you.

- **Practice kindness.** I know being kind to yourself might feel like an impossible task at the moment, but anything can make a difference. Acknowledging the fact that you cleaned your teeth or changed your pyjamas or went to work despite feeling like shit is a step in the right direction, even if you can't outright congratulate yourself for it.

- **Go outside.** Sometimes, there's no prison quite as suffocating as your own four walls and getting out of the house can help offer a slight shift in perspective. I don't believe that this is a fix-all but a change of scenery and a break in routine can mix things up enough to help you see a bit more clearly.

- **Swim.** This is one which is very personal to me and I know not everyone will feel the same but I never know clarity more than when I am in water. There's something about recognising my body for the great things it is able to do and offer me that really resonates with me when I'm not feeling ship-shape mentally. If you ever need reminding that you're alive, that your home is a human body that does great things every single day without trying, that your overactive and critical mind is just a byproduct of evolution, find some water. The colder the better. Hear your breath, feel the flutter of the gentle waves over your ears, taste the chlorine or the salt or the nature on the tip of your tongue, count your strokes, your lengths, your minutes in the water. Float. And try not to feel a bit more like you're living the best life you can - even if it's just for the time you're swimming.

• **Read.** I read a lot. You can't be a writer without being a reader. So our house is packed to the rafters with book after book after book, the words and stories of brilliant writers who fill my life with different perspectives and help me learn about experiences and I'm lucky that my depression rarely hinders my ability to shut myself off from the real world by firmly placing my nose in a book. If I'm in a bad place though, I turn to creature comforts, the classics of my youth that will always offer my heart a protective shell - like JK Rowling's Harry Potter and Goodnight Mr Tom by Michelle Magorian. I've also popped a list of other books I've found that have offered me solace in the resources section of the epilogue of this book.

• **Write.** Many mental health experts recommend writing or journaling to help improve your mood and manage symptoms of depression. The process helps you get to know yourself better, lets you reframe your experiences and can help you notice patterns, leading to identifying any triggers. Again, it's not a cure-all but for many people (me included) writing things down helps them figure out how they feel about life and this clarity can be crucial to recognising depressive feelings. I've started keeping a journal recently, and it's not like the old days of professing my love for a particular boy in my science class or complaining because my friends didn't sit with me at lunch - it has just become a way for me to unload some of the many, many things going on in my life at any one time.

• **Meditate.** I was incredibly lucky to have been offered an MCBT (Mindful Cognitive Behavioural Therapy) course on the NHS to learn how to meditate and explore how mindfulness can assist with a brain that's constantly fizzing with overzealous thoughts and feelings. I wrote a piece for Stylist on this explaining "It's certainly far from an overnight fix - doing mindfulness in this way when you're already predisposed to excessive rumination can make things worse before it makes things better, but there's irrefutable evidence that mindfulness isn't just a buzzword. According to recent research, mindfulness-based cognitive therapy (MBCT) can help people just as much as commonly prescribed antidepressant drugs. Not only that, but the research found those who received MCBT were 31% less likely to experience a relapse of their depression." So give it a try. But exercise caution and seek guidance

• **Breathe.** If meditation feels too hippy dippy and far out to you, sometimes just stopping, closing your eyes and taking a deep breath through your nose can be enough to reset and stop your thoughts from running away with you. Try and breathe right down into your belly, taking the time to feel your lungs fill up from the very bottom. Feel your belly expand. Feel the breath really fill you up. Exhale slowly, by making it as long as your inhale. Just doing this a few times can be enough to stop negative thought patterns that can lead to increased anxiety or depressive episodes in their tracks.

• **Talk.** I've written about this before, but if talking is something that feels right to you, it's worth trying to do. Not everyone is able to talk about their issues but if you feel comfortable doing it, it can be a massive salvation. You don't have to seek professional help (though I'd suggest it's always worth a try), even just chatting to a close friend or family member can help lighten your load. A problem shared and all that. Don't be afraid of therapists though - there's nothing better than having a safe place in which you can talk freely with no fear of repercussions, hurting anyone's feelings or scaring anyone off. I'd also add that if you've tried a therapist and they didn't work for you, try another one. It's a really important relationship and getting the right person is a crucial part of ensuring you get what you need out of it. Don't be afraid to do exactly what YOU need to get the most out of the experience.

• **Exercise.** It's the old favourite. The "exercise is good for mental health" schtick does piss me off sometimes, but the truth is, it really can make a difference. A brisk walk, a yoga class, a run, punching a bag at Boxfit, dancing your heart out at a Zumba class or going hell for leather at Spin can have a huge positive impact on your mental health - but I'd argue that these things are more of a preventative measure than a solution that will drag you from the depths. After all, if you can't face getting out of bed, how are you going to drag yourself to the gym? But cultivating an exercise practice that works for you can keep those depressive spells and anxious thoughts at bay.

• **Learn.** I read a passage in *The Observer* in February 2018 (How I beat anorexia by savouring the lavish meals of literature by Sarah Hughes) with author of *The Reading Cure*, Laura Freeman, and found the following passage exceptionally pertinent: "I really loved TH White's *The Once and Future King*" she says, "in particular Merlin's advice to his young apprentice, Wart, that whenever you're low or sad, the thing that never fails, the thing you have absolute control of, is to teach yourself something, learn something new. It made me realise that when I am having a bad day - and they do come around - I can go to a museum, read a book, or go for a walk. I can fill my brain with something that isn't my own nitty gritty unhappiness". Don't know about you, pals but this makes absolute, total and complete sense to me.

• **Rest**. You've heard the expression "learn to rest, not to quit"? It tends to be seen on super intense fitspiration blogs and Instagram accounts which have slightly aggressive undertones, but I think it's generally a good message for managing your mental health. If you're feeling exhausted by battles with your brain, resting is totally key. There's a balance between resting too much and not enough, but only you can really be the judge of that (and trust the kind voice in your head, not the gremlin who is telling you you're lazy). Netflix is your friend and key for self preservation. I recommend copious amounts of Gilmore Girls.

• **Eat something delicious and nutritious.** You deserve nutrition even if you don't feel like it. You deserve to eat something even if you don't feel like it. Don't judge yourself if all you can do is muster the energy to put the kettle on and make a pot noodle, but try for something a bit more nutritious if you can because food has all sorts of great properties that can help with your mood. There is absolutely no way I am going to tell you to go sugar free, because unfortunately, that is against my religion but lean proteins, whole grains, fresh fruits and vegetables, and fish are sometimes billed as "good mood foods" which can increase energy levels and improve mental focus - helping you get out of a slump. An excellent accompaniment to healthy food is a tasty biscuit or chocolate bar. And calories just equal delicious points. The act of cooking in itself can be meditative and an excellent exercise in self care too if done right. Taking time out of life to prepare yourself food is a great way to remind yourself you deserve some TLC if you can find the energy to. The kitchen can be a safe place if you need it to be. (NB - I realise this isn't always the case as people can have many issues with food, but I think the key thing to remember is that you DESERVE to be nourished, no matter what your brain is telling you.

• **Get a hug.** There are SO many benefits to hugging. According to MindBodyGreen (*10 Reasons Why We Need at Least 8 Hugs a Day*, Marcus Julian Felicetti), research shows that a proper deep hug, where the hearts are pressing together can be hugely beneficial, with positives including an increased oxytocin levels which can help with healing feelings of loneliness, isolation, and anger; increased serotonin levels; released tension within the body, boosted self esteem and tonnes more. If you can't get a hug from someone else, giving yourself a squeeze can be beneficial too, and in case you're wondering how best to do this, there's a WikiHow for that (ACTUALLY). You can also buy "therapeutic blankets" which are designed to reduce stress and anxiety by simulating the sensation of being hugged. Yes please.

• **Seek help**: If you're in crisis and really struggling, don't hesitate to call your doctors and ask for an emergency appointment. If you are thinking about hurting yourself or someone else, go straight to A&E. Someone from your GP team should be able to see or speak to you on the same day if you ask to, or if that's not available they should be able to signpost you to another local service. They may suggest a walk in clinic, mental health services or A&E local to you.There are also a number of helplines you can call if you're in distress, including

The Samaritans on 116 123 (available 24/7);
Mind on 0300 123 3393 (available 9am - 6pm Monday - Friday);
CALM for men on 0800 58 58 58 (available 5pm - Midnight every day);
The Mix for under 25s on 0808 808 4994 (available 24/7)

• **Lastly, remember - you're doing the best you can**

im sorry alice its cancer

Chapter 5: Early Days of Cancer

Within days of being diagnosed, I'd returned to my hometown in North Yorkshire, told all of the people I needed to tell in a haze, convinced I was making the whole thing up, and stumbled back down to London for further tests. Had Chris not been by my side the day they told me it was cancer, I think I would have convinced myself that this was my brain playing tricks on me in some warped attempt to get attention. Alas, as I was moved from test to test I had to accept that wasn't the case and I did, in fact, have cancer. Even as the words felt like staples in my mouth, I had to start the process of accepting that they were true. The appointments for all of the tests had been made for me as if the NHS were a well-oiled, perfectly well-staffed and perfectly well-funded machine that was not remotely in crisis. I was grateful for the list I was presented with that told me where I had to be and when I had to be there.

There was a contrast mammogram, where a dye that is kept at room temperature is injected into your veins. Why am I telling you the temperature of the dye? Because, APPARENTLY if you have something injected into your veins which is kept at room temperature, the warmth has a tendency to rush to all of your extremities, making you feel distinctly like you've wet yourself. True story. Literally 30 seconds after they'd injected the dye through a cannula in my right arm, I had to do a pat down to make sure I hadn't had a little wee (you'll be glad to know that cancer hadn't suddenly caused me to become incontinent). Contrast mammograms are a key diagnostic tool for breast cancer in younger women. Our breast tissue is more dense than that of older women, so it's harder to see if there's any cancer lurking about on a regular mammogram. The contrast mammo provides medics with a clearer picture, often spotting cancers that may not be visible on regular mammograms.

I had another ultrasound on both my cancer-ridden boob and the boob that was more well behaved to establish whether there was any cancer anywhere else. They'd found another lump too, so needed to ultrasound and biopsy that to make sure there was no nastiness in there and the radiologist asked Chris to leave the room while she carried out the biopsy. She told him I was her priority, it wasn't a pleasant procedure to witness and the last thing she needed was to have to deal with him passed out on the floor. Part of me felt like I could get used to being everybody's priority, but I would definitely have passed up on the ole cancer if it meant not being anyone's main concern.

I was also scheduled for an MRI. Little did I know but the aim of this MRI was to establish the stage of my cancer, notably if it had spread anywhere beyond my breast. At this point, I was still learning the language of breast cancer. I had no idea that cancer could travel beyond my breast, and make its home in the other parts of my body. I've spoken to other people who had their MRI scans and then spent the weeks following anxiously awaiting the news of whether the tumourous cells had settled anywhere else, meaning that the cancer was incurable and terminal. I was oblivious to this. Oblivious to the fact that this was even a thing they'd be checking for. That naivety saved me though. Now I long for the time when I didn't know about secondary breast cancer, when the thought of the cancer returning and spreading didn't plague my thoughts. At the time, I was more preoccupied by claustrophobia and the decision of the MRI team to play Fields of Gold by Eva Cassidy while I was in the tube being scanned for cancer. Yep. They played the CANCER SONG while scanning a person for cancer. Honestly, I feel like they didn't think that through well at all?

As well as tests, I had appointments with a tonne of medical professionals. I met with a Genetics Counsellor, so I could be tested for the BRCA gene (the two genes which, if mutated, greatly increase an individual's chance of developing breast and ovarian cancer in their lifetime). I met my oncology team for the first time. I met with fertility professionals to consider ways to protect my fertility, because treatment can ravage your reproductive system. The Assisted Conception Unit is a pretty bleak place. We were easily the youngest couple in there, and I've never felt more like I was in a place where dreams were made or crushed than sitting in that waiting room. I watched as couples made their way out of the room in tears or with tentative smiles on their faces. They were literally putting their hearts on the line to try to make a family and I felt like an imposter. I've never really wanted kids, but here I was being forced to consider my fertility in the most assaulting way. If I think back to that time, (which I do frequently, because cancer and fertility have become inextricably linked in my mind) my memory is so hazy. A friend of mine recently went through fertility treatment and she asked me what it was like, how much of each injection I had, how many follicles I had, how many eggs they retrieved - and I couldn't tell her. I guess at the time, despite how massive a part of my cancer treatment protecting my fertility was, it wasn't a priority for me.

The early days of cancer were and remain a bit of a blur. I went from work meetings talking about moneysaving and marketing to talking about hormone injections, eggs and embryos. I went from my most important decision being what to make for dinner, to deciding whether I wanted chemotherapy first, or surgery first and establishing which one gave me a better chance of survival. I went from being an average 20-something Londoner who was going out for dinners and hanging out at music festivals to trying to save my own life.

I think it took a while for the cancer news to sink in, but two weeks after my diagnosis, I met the surgeon who would go on to save my life, and carry out more surgeries on me than either of us would care to remember. I hadn't actually cried about cancer all that much. I'd had a bit of a weep here and there, but I think the shock of my diagnosis meant that I hadn't really processed it. No matter how many times you tell yourself "I've got breast cancer" it still doesn't really seem all that real. But apparently when you're sat on the 521 from London Bridge to Waterloo having just agreed to have your entire right breast removed in less than two weeks, and someone sends you a really bloody nice email, that's when it hits you. Then you start to sob a little bit and then the sodding flood-gates open and you're not sure you're ever actually going to stop crying.

I did stop crying. Eventually. But I needed to give in. To let that emotion leave me. I think that was the day cancer stopped being a weird and disjointed nightmare to me and became the reality I was facing over the next 10 months. The tears came as I was overpowered by all of the nervous energy, fear, exhaustion and general emotion of the previous two weeks and flooded out in every direction. The tears came because I'd just made one of the biggest decisions of my adult life.

There was never any question for me though, really. As I sat in front of my surgeon, King K (name changed to protect the innocent and offer him an ego boost, should he ever read this book and need it, HA), the first time I met him, discussing my options, I was presented with a choice. I was in a pretty unique position. The location of my tumour meant that I had a choice as to how we proceeded. He told me that if he had two versions of me standing in front of him, and he gave one a mastectomy, and one a lumpectomy, the results would be much the same, but the

Alice who had a mastectomy stood less chance of the aggressive cancer that had made it's home in my body coming back. From where I was sitting, there was no choice. When faced with reducing the chances of my (already likely to recur) cancer recurring, a nipple-sparing mastectomy with immediate reconstruction was the only option.

In a whirlwind of moments, my surgery was scheduled for 3rd August 2015. Just a matter of weeks after diagnosis. My mastectomy was to become my first ever surgery. The first time I'd ever had an anaesthetic. Way to go in at the deep-end, right?

I don't think I've ever been as scared as I was on the morning of my mastectomy. My heart relocated to my stomach as I was marked up, a massive arrow drawn on the right hand side of my chest to indicate which breast was the troublesome one. I felt my breath becoming tight and anxious as a cannula was inserted into my veins. One of the nurses, sensing my vulnerability, took a moment to squeeze my hand. That squeeze was like a life raft being thrown to me as I was drowning. I wonder how I would have felt if I'd known that this was the first in what would very quickly become a long series of surgeries spanning over three years.

The thing about anaesthetic, if you've never had one, is that you fall under its spell and feel like you wake up seconds later, usually a bit confused, very nauseous, often cold, occasionally chatting total rubbish and generally flummoxed that you could possibly have had life-changing surgery in the 20 seconds you were asleep. Every time I've come round from anaesthetic (and it's been a few, more on that to come, you lucky devils), it's felt like a click of fingers has passed between counting down from ten to the nurse gently calling my name and asking me how I'm feeling. It's like some kind of magic.

It was a straightforward procedure. One that King K had carried out countless times before. In an effort to save my nipple, they cut a line from under the armpit side of my chest and under the nipple, pulled out all of the breast tissue, replacing it with a tear-drop shaped implant that aimed to mimic the shape of a regular breast. I went to sleep with cancer. I woke up without it. And that was quite something.

After the surgery, I was kept in hospital for two nights. Having been discharged in time for the new series of Great British Bake Off, I left the hospital with a shoulder bag that carried two bottles of my bodily fluids - drains to remove the serous fluid from the surgical site. And that should have been it for my surgical procedures. But it wasn't.

I left the hospital bruised, battered, unable to wash myself properly. The drain bottles, attached to me via a thin tube of PVC, were far removed from the luxurious Cambridge Satchel Co handbag I was used to toting round, but at least they were popped in a little floral handbag so the outside world didn't need to know what I was carrying round with me. Well, until I displayed the bottles to anyone who expressed even the slightest bit of interest. Even those who didn't. My bloody bodily fluids, complete with the clots in the serous fluid, floating around like little brains have been seen by far more people than you'd imagine. No shame here.

The chronology of events after that surgery are lost on me now. Part of me wishes I'd kept tighter hold of the moments as they unfolded, gripping onto the strands of experience that made up the events of those early days, but hindsight is a wonderful thing and my memory of my cancer experience is vague in the way I expect the memory of childbirth is vague. Perhaps it is a self preservation thing. My brain's way of protecting me from the experiences. But the following few months were fairly traumatic.

A few weeks after my mastectomy I tried to make it back into the office and regain some semblance of normality in one of the most turbulent times of my life, determined to keep working as much as I could, but my body had other ideas. The skin around my scar was refusing to heal. I stepped off the busy commuter train at 9am on a bustling London morning, my chest (literally) heavy with the weight of the implant, and pulled my coat around me. It was damp. Everything was damp. My dress was soaked. Sodden. Serous fluid had begun to leak through the surgical scar left behind from my mastectomy as it struggled to hold together. And the thing about when you've had a breast reconstruction is that if stuff is coming out of your scar, stuff can get in, meaning your risk of infection is heightened. I frantically called my breast care nurse and she told me to make my way to the hospital urgently. Through the tears and snot that had already begun, I managed to order an Uber and then call my father. Despite the state I was in I still managed to tell the Uber driver to have a lovely day, as he dropped me off at the hospital probably wondering what in God's name was happening. MANNERS COST NOTHING, GUYS.

I was admitted to the day surgery unit at my hospital, for the first of several attempts to save the implant that had replaced the tumour and the other tissue in my breast. King K sewed me up and sent me on my way, hopeful that a few stitches would help the skin knit together and heal. But my body was clearly tired. My immune system was already struggling to do what it needed to do to protect me and once again, the skin refused to heal.

I call this section of my life The Ballad of the Exploding Breast, but events merge into one another and there are some significant blank spots where I've clearly blacked out events like my brain is trying to protect me from myself. There were four times when I was rushed into surgery to try to restitch the scar and force the skin to heal. I had a new implant inserted every time. We tried smaller silicone implants, an expander implant (which is basically a pocket filled with saline via a port to increase volume) at 50% filled. Then with nothing in it. Just an empty pocket with rigid edges that crumpled and reshaped and stung my skin from the inside. And with the early surgeries, starting chemo was pushed back, until my body was healed and ready.

It sounds like a weird thing to say, but I was craving chemotherapy by this point. If there's one thing I'm not good with it is uncertainty and the fact that no-one could tell me exactly how I was going to react on chemo, if I was going to be able to work, if it was going to make me sick, filled me with dread. I just wanted to get it started so that I could get it finished, but every surgery, every complication with healing meant it was taken further and further away from me. Eventually, I was deemed healed enough to begin my chemotherapy regime, but after both of my first two cycles, I quickly became neutropenic. My body didn't have enough white blood cells to fight infection, making me incredibly susceptible to sepsis, genuinely putting my life at risk. I was admitted to hospital with yet another infection in my breast as the skin that we thought had healed around my surgical scar became dark as it died. It was the same again. Fluid coming out. Risk of infection and losing the implant.

The neutropenia made me frail and empty and led to me throwing up in the tiniest bin you've ever seen and then again in a recycling bin. I am still plagued by the thought of the person who found those sick-filled bins but grateful that I'd only managed to eat an apple beforehand. And to be honest, my biggest concern was that the hospital would get charged for the wrong materials being put into the recycling bins. Every bin in the hospital has a notice affixed to the front, saying what should go in it, with a harshly worded message to say that any of the incorrect items in the recycling bins would lead to fines for the trust. I'm pretty sure "vomit" wasn't included as a correct material for the paper recycling bin. Alas, I'll never know if the hospital was fined. Nor will I ever know who had to clean up my sick after me. But if you're reading this and you work at Guy's Hospital and cleaned vomit out of a semi-circle bin near the lifts on the fourth floor sometime in October 2015, it was probably my fault. Sorry about that.

Anyway. It reached a point where I was beyond exhausted. The skin had refused to heal time and time again. Once again there was liquid flowing from my body in places it shouldn't have been. One of the key memories I have of this time was one Sunday night where serous fluid was pouring from my scar, so much so that I couldn't stand up without a river cascading down my torso. Chris grabbed literally every dressing that we had in the house and layered them on to try and deal with the flow until we could get to the breast clinic the next day. The pile of dressings thrown on transformed my right breast from a double D cup to about a J cup. But it was all we could do. We laughed at how utterly absurd that whole situation was. We cried a little that this had happened once more.

Once again my surgeon wanted to stitch me up but I was sick of surgeries. Between August and October 2015, I'd had at least one operation a month. The emotional turmoil of thinking I'd healed only to discover that I hadn't was too much for my brain to cope with as I was dealing with all the other side effects of treatment – the mental, the physical and the medical. I told him I was done. I asked him to take the implant out. He did.

Less than three months after having a mastectomy with an immediate reconstruction, I was left with a crater. An empty space where a huge part of my femininity had been. Now I'd truly lost my breast – and with it, a massive part of myself.

It's mad to me that the Ballad of the Exploding breast unfolded within two months of my diagnosis. What should have been a relatively straightforward thing, turned out not to be as my body refused to do as it was being asked. The demands on it were too much, it seems. So the early days of cancer were more tumultuous than I would have liked. Not only was I getting to grips with my body failing me in the most dramatic way possible, by turning against me and growing cancerous cells rather than healthy ones, it was letting me down by not doing its part in my survival. We went through some pretty tempestuous times, my body and I at that time. We were certainly not seeing eye to eye.

But after the implant was removed, things began to level out a bit and I established some sense of normality in the crazy world of living with a cancer diagnosis. As with all of my cancer experience, it wasn't all doom and gloom. I got a prosthetic and named her Gladys. I got a Knitted Knocker and called her Knit Tit. I got a prosthetic for swimming and named her Rebecca Adlington. I cried when I bought the massive mastectomy bras designed to hold these replacement boobs in position, but I cried with laughter when I realised the aqua prosthetic made a vacuum and stuck to the wall with the right amount of pressure. On my wedding day, when my heavy prosthetic was sweaty and uncomfortable, I grappled around in my bra and whipped Gladys out. I shouted my friend across the room, warned her to think fast and launched the chicken fillet type breast prosthesis directly at her.

Every part of cancer treatment brings some kind of life lesson. I know how cliched that sounds. I kind of hate myself for saying it, but the early days of cancer taught me that I was better prepared for adversity than I realised. It also taught me that when immense pressure is applied to Christopher John Newman, he has an exceptionally strong stomach for Terry's Chocolate Oranges and a remarkable aptitude for four to six hour panic naps.

And what of my brain in all of this? How was that guy coping with the Ballad of the Exploding Breast? How was it dealing with the fact that my body was trying to kill me? How was it managing to process the trauma of what my body was going through? How was it preparing for the eventuality of chemo? How was it dealing with the fear of the unknown? Had I even processed that I could die as a result of this? The honest answer is I have no idea. I don't know how I managed. I've no idea how I got up every day and carried on. Those days were some of the darkest I've ever experienced, but not in the same way I'd known the darkness of depression. I was physically and emotionally empty, unable to feel anything other than an unrelenting darkness that hit me right in the stomach and stopped me from living for days at a time. Were these the feelings of anyone going through cancer treatment or was it exacerbated by my already negatively inclined brain? It's impossible to say, but I find it hard to imagine that the two were not linked, with the cancer experience exacerbating the blues that I was so used to.

I look back on my blogposts for the time just after I was diagnosed, those early days of cancer and see a terrified young woman who is desperately trying to keep her head above the water by making jokes and "staying positive". But I know she was terrified. And she was lost. And she was consumed by darkness and fear. I know she described having cancer as "a bit of a shame" and "a bit of an inconvenience" but that person was hiding a lot of pain and suffering. Part self-preservation, part protection for those around her.

The person I was before cancer almost feels like a stranger to me now. If I had to describe myself before and after cancer, I'd say it's like I am a twin of the person I was before. The same, but so very, very different. I look the same, for the most part. My views are the same (if not a little more…strident). But my hopes and dreams are different. My day-to-day is different. My outlook on life is fundamentally changed. I'm the same person as I was then, but I'm so very different. The person I was during cancer feels like a stranger to me too. I have been broken into pieces, not even whole pieces, shards of pieces, and I have, with the love of those around me (as well as really quite a lot of therapy - I love the NHS!) put myself back together. I'm still a work in progress. Someone told me I had been through hellfire and I still have the burns. I do. They were third degree burns that threatened my existence. But every day is like a new skin graft, plastering over the cracks and giving new strength. Those early days of cancer are a long way away from me now. And still not so far away at all. I am still a work in progress.

But then, aren't we all, cancer or no cancer. Depression or no depression.

13 Things You Discover if You're Being Treated for Breast cancer

The world changes a bit when you hear those words "it's cancer" – but not necessarily for the worst. It's a steep learning curve, but one with lots of highs to counteract the pretty rubbishy lows. Here's 13 things you know if you're being treated for breast cancer.

1. Your emotions are completely out of your control. When you wake up in the morning and think "I have GOT THIS today" you can't guarantee that by the end of the day, you won't be a quivering mess of snot and tears who was floored by putting a load of washing in.

2. You're conflicted over whether or not to eat all of the food or just stick to fruit and veg. You know the whole "sugar feeds cancer" thing is a myth (and you listen to the people in the hospital – you know, the professionals, rather than trusting what you read on the Internet) but you still feel just a leeeeeeetle bit guilty when you eat a handful of Nerds you bought in a nostalgic throwback to your youth, or when the only thing that makes your furry chemo tongue temporarily tolerable is a steady diet of fizzy strawberry laces.

3. You feel all of the guilt. Even though you KNOW getting breast cancer was not your fault, you feel bad for inconveniencing the surgeon when your boob springs a leak and you feel bad that your long suffering boyfriend/friend/parent/sibling is labelled as your carer because something decided to mutate in your body

4. You can't concentrate on any of the amazing books you've bought/been sent in preparation for your recuperation, so you

end up re-reading Harry Potter. I mean – this isn't a bad thing. Obvs.

5. When recovering from surgery, you realise just how short an episode of Sex and the City is, when you accidentally watch a whole season in a day without really thinking about it, and only stop for meals or a brisk walk around the park.

6. You miss exercise and you almost don't recognise yourself as a result. Four years ago, you'd not have even sniffed at eight weeks of an enforced reduction in your usual exercise routine. Truth be told, you'd probably barely have even noticed. Surgery takes away your ability to run, swim and do yoga. So you're stuck to combatting cabin fever with those brisk walks around the park and Netflix marathons instead of actual running.

7. You have a deep rooted and intense appreciation of the NHS. Even though you've always known it's the absolute cats pyjamas, the treatment you've received is second to none and your gratitude knows no bounds. If you could, you'd give every medical professional you meet a hug or a high five and you'd even be willing to pay higher taxes so more people can experience the quality of care you've received at the most tricky time of your life.

8. You find humour in the most unlikely of places. Like in the assisted conception unit when you end up dressing like you work in a cheese factory, or when you joke about what Halloween costumes you'll be able to rock when chemo has made your hair fall out. When you try on wigs with stripper names like "Candy" and you get teased for the way you laugh when you're on morphine. (8.1 – it is these moments that keep you sane).

9. Your boobs (actually your body) will pretty much become public

property. You'll be surprised at how quickly you get used to having serious conversations with your knockers out, and how little you care about who sees your boobs in a clinical setting.

10. You feel like you talk about cancer literally 24/7 and you'd give anything for cancer to be removed from your vocabulary/memory Eternal Sunshine style for just a couple of hours. You surprise yourself when you realise you haven't thought about cancer for a couple of hours, or more impressively, if you manage to temporarily forget you've got the thing and carry on your day like normal.

11. You end up making new friends who are also on this mad (X Factor word) journey. Again your inhibitions are completely discarded and you find yourself chatting with them openly about your boobs, drug side effects (including bowel movements), and your fears and thoughts on this whole alien experience. Though you wish to god these people you've come to care about quite a lot, very quickly, didn't have to have cancer, you're kind of glad you've got them to go through this with.

12. There will be bad days but there will be a LOT of good days too. More than you expected when you heard those words "it is cancer". And you'll surprise yourself with how resilient you are to shitty news and crappy circumstances. You'll find the good bits in pretty much every day and, true to the cliche, you'll think more about the stuff that's important than ever before and stop sweating the stuff that pales in comparison.

13. Just how lucky you are to have such a solid bunch of people around you. Just how loved and supported you will feel by your family and the friends you have chosen as family. They'll give you strength when your outlook is dark and they'll let you cry when you need to, laugh when you should and make the whole process of kicking the heck out of cancer that much easier.

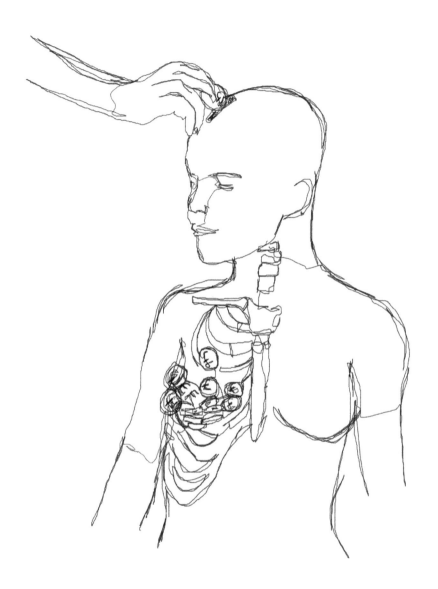

Chapter 6: Am I worth it?

If there's one thing you find yourself with an abundance of during cancer treatment, it's spare time. Usually, the vast majority of this spare time is spent alone too, while you go about the business of being unwell and your family, friends, loved ones - pretty much all of the people you know - go about the business of winning bread and earning a living. Time can be a luxury. Time can be an opportunity to catch up on the things you've been neglecting (I think of Rachel in 90's classic *Friends* "catching up on her correspondence" as a way to avoid going to a ball with Ross after he pissed her off); it's a chance to binge-watch terrible American sitcoms (I'm looking at you, *Pretty Little Liars*), or bake delicious treats, or devour the words of writers you admire. But for many with depression, time alone can be more of a curse than a blessing. There's nothing harder than dealing with the deafening thoughts of your own mind if there's nothing to distract you, nothing to drown out the rallying cries telling you that you're a disappointment and you're letting everyone down.

On one of these days where my mind was overactive and bordering on the unhealthy side of that overactivity while I was in treatment, I saw a post on The Guardian that piqued my interest. I know I should have avoided it. In my right mind, I can forsee the impact this kind of news article would have on my mental state. My right mind practically races towards me and rips the phone out of my hand, throws it across the room and shouts "DO A CROSSWORD INSTEAD ALICE." But when I'm more volatile and vulnerable it's harder to see those things, the warning signs, the markers of things best avoided. I can't remember the headline of the article, but I remember it stopped me in my tracks as I scrolled through Facebook (another pastime which is probably best avoided if you're in the midst of a blue mist). It was a calculator which estimated the amount of money an individual had cost the NHS. It asked you to select the treatments you'd had, from GP appointments, to meetings with specialists, surgeries, medications - practically everything you can think of. I spent some time entering all the things our beloved and beleaguered NHS had paid for me to have. The cost was astronomical and didn't even include all of the surgeries I'd had after my mastectomy. It didn't include all of the medication I'd been given to stem the nausea and deal with the pain of being cut open and having my breast tissue removed. There was no mention of the cost of multiple implants that had been inserted under my skin, nor was I able to realistically estimate the number of appointments I'd had with the surgeon who refused to let anyone else see me. It didn't mention the fertility treatment, or the Zoladex injections I'd had to shut my ovaries down and protect my chance of having kids in the future. As I totted up the estimated costs I had incurred for the NHS, I felt sick. This estimate was definitely on the lower side of reality and it was still mind-blowing. The sickness became guilt as I wondered what I had done to deserve to have the hard-earned money of the nation's tax payers spent on me. I was in a bad place at the time, scared and worried and broken and exhausted. I didn't feel like I wanted to keep going. And the question of whether I was wasting that money and costing the struggling NHS because I didn't deserve it rang through my head like a particularly shrill and unpleasant sounding doorbell. Shouldn't I really, really, want to live to make it worth it? Can I actually tell anyone that I don't know if I want to live when so much time, energy and effort is being exerted with the sole intention of saving my life?

The cost of cancer treatment is phenomenal. I dread to think what I would have had to pay had I not been lucky enough to be born in the UK in the time of the NHS (I'm just sayin' if Walter White had been British, Breaking Bad would never have happened and he would never have needed to become Heisenberg). Still, I felt (feel) pretty sheepish that so much of that money was spent on me when I've never really felt like I deserve it.

The truth is, when I was in the throes of treatment, a lot of the time I felt like I didn't deserve to live. I felt like my card had been marked and thus any "fight" was futile. I never felt like I deserved to get cancer, but equally, I didn't feel like I didn't deserve it either. My little brain gremlin told me that of course I was going to get cancer because why should a lousy person like me be allowed to live a healthy, stress-free life? I don't know whether my mental health issues were exacerbated by my experience of cancer, or whether that was just a catalyst for the downfall that was on the way anyway, but things got really bleak there for a while. And I know there are plenty of other people who have been through cancer treatment who would say the same, but I experienced some of the very darkest days of my life when I was in cancer treatment. I don't want to go into them in detail here because I don't think it's beneficial for you to hear the thoughts I had at that time. It adds no value to the story or to my life or your life to talk about the bleakness of those times. But it is important to recognise that these feelings occur.

Anyone could be hit by a bus at any time, but facing my mortality at 26 was something I struggled with, and something I continue to consider. As I sit here now, three years since diagnosis and almost three years since finishing treatment, I still think about dying more than I ever did before I got sick. It has become less over time and I suppose you could argue that anyone would be more inclined to consider their own life conclusion after a serious illness - once you're reminded that you're not going to live forever, it's not something that's easy to forget. You know everyone is going to die, but getting a cancer diagnosis is like being put on notice of it happening. We definitely all take for granted that our time on this planet is finite and I know it's cliched to say it, getting diagnosed with cancer really is a wakeup call - a reminder that you are not invincible, impervious to disease. And it happening before you're even 30 is a pretty big kick in the mouth of reality, I think. My cancer "experience" (which I have written a million times in this book and on my blog and across various other spaces for the written word and which still never feels like the right way to describe the clusterfuck) gave me all kinds of feelings about wanting to do more with my life but my depression made me expect myself to do all of these things immediately, otherwise I was a massive failure. Obviously.

But it's interesting that so many people are scared of talking and thinking about death. Being presented with the fact that I wasn't going to live forever in such an undeniable way has given me so much to run around with in my little brain. We are all guilty of pretending that death is something that will never happen to us, when in fact, it's one of the very few certainties in life. So why shouldn't we confront it? Why not talk about what you want to happen when you die, whether you're facing it tomorrow (which one could argue we all are, especially if you ever try to cross a road in London) or further down the line. Not long after I finished treatment, I wrote Chris a note and tucked it away in a book that told him exactly what I wanted to happen if I did cark it sooner rather than later. I left it in the book *The Year of Magical Thinking* by Joan Didion (definitely a must read if you have ever experienced grief of any kind - whether for a loved one or for yourself and the person you used to be). My views have changed a bit since then so I probably need to update the card but I now have a pretty clear idea of what I want to happen when my days on this earth are done. I would never have had that without cancer. I also sat down and wrote a will not so long ago. The question (to paraphrase) "what would you like to happen to your estate if you and your family all die together?" was not a particularly nice one to ponder and it felt inordinately grown up but it was part of a pretty crucial process. All of this served as a reminder that death is not something to fear. It's the other side of life. Nothing is more certain and therefore, we need to face it head on. Having cancer has removed any uneasiness around death I may have had before. I make jokes about it now, in a way I never would have, had I not been forced to look my own mortality in its grizzly face.

At the times in treatment where I felt like I no longer wanted to live, I think I had simply and completely run out of energy. I have never experienced exhaustion like I felt during my cancer treatment. I still get tired, but there were times when I couldn't even walk ten minutes to the shop without needing a nap when I got there, and the fish aisle of the local Co-Op is not the optimum place to catch some Z's. This exhaustion was all-encompassing, sapping me of every millilitre of "fight" I had in me. And there are so many similarities here with the lowest of the low feeling that comes with depression. The impact of both of these things are so hugely underrated, but I genuinely feel that a huge part of my suicidal ideation (at worst) or my wishes to just not exist any more (at best) tend to come from a place of total and complete burnout, whether mental, physical or a combination of the two. While I was in chemo, I was burned out by the process of getting better, by the idea that to make myself better I had to go through all of these gruelling procedures that were making me more ill than I had ever felt. I was tired of doctor's appointments, I was tired of waking up every morning and knowing that there were more challenges ahead than I knew what to do with. I was tired of the new symptoms and the new side effects, the blisters in my nose, the numbness in my fingers, the cracking skin around my eyeballs. It was these things that made it feel like I couldn't bear to keep going another day. Because would it all be worth it? And how could I guarantee that if I did keep going, the blues that had so often pervaded my life wouldn't come and do the job cancer had already tried to do? Not only that but I had lost myself and I couldn't see a way back to being a human who had value and purpose. I saw myself as a patient and a useless human. Because in case you hadn't noticed, that's what I tell myself a lot of the time when I'm struggling.

There's something to be said for science and biology and the way the brain is wired, but I think a lot of my mental health issues (cancer carefully put to one side for the time being) come back to exhaustion too. Not in the sense of the word as just being overly tired. But the pure, unrelenting exhaustion that sometimes comes from existing in the modern world. From when the news is filled with terrible things that are happening across the globe and you feel like the world is crumbling around you, to the pressure of looking and being a certain way that is prescribed by companies made to sell products. Constantly striving to do better, to be better, to create more, to make the most of every opportunity thrown your way for fear of not making the most of this wild gift of life we've been given. Modern life is so tricky to navigate, we're all constantly grappling for solutions and quick fixes to make the whole thing seem a bit less overwhelming. All of that is amplified ten thousand fold when you throw cancer into the mix as well, especially if you're inclined to overthink things anyway.

Over the last few years, I have watched a lot of Grey's Anatomy. I discovered it was on Amazon Prime and I started watching it from the beginning. Some people say it's depressing but in those early days, the dialogue was quick-witted, sharp, moving and funny, while the storylines pushed the boundaries of medicine and beyond. You'd think given the amount of time I've spent in a hospital and given the fact that my own hospital gives me palpitations every time I visit, I'd want nothing to do with a medical drama. Sometimes I don't. But as with most things I find comfort in the familiar and the old storylines and well-worn characters offer me some kind of safe space. A space in which I can exist without my mind for a while. It's chewing gum for the brain, with a heart.

Obviously watching Greys, you see a lot of surgical scenes. You see amputated limbs and gore and loss and the medical terminology washes over you like a second language you're almost fluent in. You hear talk of scalpels and defibrillators and "apis" and sutures. Sutures. That's the one I have become fixated on of late.

When I had the tiny cyst removed from my left breast when I was 19, I remember asking them how many stitches they had used. There were eight of them, I think. I'd never had so much as a cut really, before then. Nothing more than a papercut. So I was fascinated by the idea that these little stitches had been put in my body to tie up the loose ends of my skin and help them knit back together. Now, obviously, I have had my fair share of sutures. I have been cut open and sewn back up almost too many times to count in the last three years. I have had little stitches over little holes and lots of bigger stitches over bigger holes. I have had the soluble type and the ones my surgeon has had to pull out and discard. I no longer know how many stitches they have put into me. I stopped asking that question once cancer was part of the equation.

But these sutures have helped my scars heal cleanly and tidily. The scar across my breast is hair thin at points – an absolute credit to the man behind the cutting and the teams behind the stitching. My chest is a battleground and the sutures were key in helping to rebuild the damage that cancer had left behind.

There are a lot of other places I could do with some sutures though. Some little stitches to help do-up the other scars that cancer has left behind. And the wounds that I leave behind on myself as a result of harsh words or criticisms or unreasonable expectations that I apply to my life. The places where I feel I am ripped open again and again – where the fear slips in and the heartache begins or where the old wounds are failing to scab over, but continue to come unstuck. There are so many parts of life that can be fixed with carefully applied medicine – sutures, or chemotherapy or radiotherapy or a hysterectomy or an appendectomy or a dose of antibiotics – but there are so many parts of life where you can't apply a sterile dressing and walk away. Where the sutures will not hold. Where a surgery cannot remove the thing that is trying to kill you.

So what can we turn to when medicine isn't enough? We try to find our own sutures for the cuts and scrapes that life throws at us. It's funny because the emotional turmoil of cancer doesn't go away, long after the tumour has gone. If you're lucky enough for the tumour to go. The emotional turmoil of cancer lingers longer than most people realise. Than I realise myself a lot of days. Sometimes I feel like I am moving forwards, sometimes I feel like I am no further ahead than I was the day I had my final radiotherapy. I am still in need of sutures, because the emotional and mental wounds that cancer left behind are pesky little blighters that keep on reopening when I least expect it. They reopen with every surgery, every hospital appointment, every lump or bump or cough or ache. Every dose of bad news. Every loss.

The wounds are healing but they never get the chance to recover completely. Because life and death and everything in between happens and we are expected to buck up and carry on. To keep getting up and keep going and be the best that we can be in this world so that our lives are not wasted. So that this chance we are given, this one life we have, can be the absolute best we can possibly make it.

No amount of sutures can heal the cuts that run much deeper than the skin and the tissue and go beyond the body. But we do the best we can.

Somehow, and I wish I could tell you how but in all honesty I have absolutely no idea, carrying on becomes the only option. It's consistently the only option. It's essentially all anyone can do. Gradually, over time, you figure out ways to stitch over the little cuts of life that can lead to big tears if you don't give them the right sort of attention and you learn to deal with whatever's thrown your way. You keep trying. You keep waking up and you keep chugging away.

We get up every day and keep doing the best we can and hope that it is enough.

It is enough. I promise it is enough.

Chapter 7: Emotions on Extra Loud

Have you ever noticed that every time someone talks about a person who's had a cancer diagnosis, any discussions usually include the words "positive" "brave" and "inspirational"? I'm yet to meet a cancer patient who doesn't find living with these adjectives attached to their personalities difficult. While I think we all appreciate that the use of these terms come from a good place, sometimes it's impossibly hard to live up to them and the expectations they elicit. I have certainly felt that to keep up the appearance of the "brave" "strong" "positive" and "inspirational" woman so many people have told me I am, there is no room for anything else. There is no room for the terror, for the pain, for the sadness, or the inappropriate jokes or the dysfunctional coping mechanisms. When we elevate people who have experienced cancer to these levels, we don't allow them the space to feel the full force of their emotions. I certainly presented a front throughout most of my treatment because I felt that showing every emotion I was feeling would have made me a failure.

Cancer brings out the very best and the very worst of the emotions in a person. There were so many days I woke up with a heavy heart, but plastered on a sunny disposition because I felt that that's what I had to do to be a good patient. To be a good person. It's something I have suffered with for a long time that doesn't just relate to cancer treatment either. Throughout most of my adult life, I have plastered a smile on and pretended everything was peachy keen when I have not wanted to exist. And living through cancer treatment was no different.

There were mornings when I woke with a list of things running through my head that were making me melancholy. There were days when I was utterly furious that cancer had chosen me. That my breast had tried to kill me. Other days I found that my emotions swung from feeling furious about my experience, to feeling nothing at all in the very depths of a hole without any walls (thanks, depression) to feeling everything all at once, on extra loud volume - to laughing and celebrating the fact I was not a carrier of the breast cancer gene but being devastated that there was no real reason for me to have breast cancer at 26. I think it's fair to say that I didn't really have a proper feeling about my diagnosis for about three months. On the day I finished chemotherapy, I wanted to be overjoyed - but I couldn't muster a single emotion. And when the day came where I felt something, I felt everything and I felt it keenly and aggressively. It felt like my brain and my skin and my mind were on fire and I was feeling everything on overdrive. There were other days where I felt positive and strong and ready to take whatever was thrown at me next - whether new side effects from the chemotherapy, the blackness of the skin as it broke down from radiotherapy or any number of the mental battles associated with life, regardless of cancer.

I have met some people who are "brave" and "inspirational" through my time in the cancer world, but I would argue that they're not that way because of the obnoxious cells that began mutating in their bodies. Kris Hallenga is "inspirational" because she used her secondary breast cancer diagnosis to create CoppaFeel! and bring about change by educating the nation on the importance of being breast aware. Her mutated cells may have been the reason for her decision, but they didn't make her into the incredible driving force she is. Jenny Baker's breast cancer cells didn't make her into the "brave" person who ran to every chemotherapy session. She already was that brave woman. Emma Cairns didn't campaign for better care for secondary breast cancer patients because the cancer cells that spread through her body gave her some kind of inspirational super power. She already had that in her. To mention my gal Sophie Trew again, creator of the UK's first holistic health and cancer awareness festival Trew Fields, she didn't magically become the inspiration she is because she was diagnosed with blood cancer. Cancer may have unlocked her potential to create the festival, but I think it's wrong to associate Sophie's achievement with being "positive" and "brave" because her body tried to kill her. She is an incredible human, regardless of her cancer experience, not BECAUSE of it.

Izzy Kennedy, Kate Lester, Lauren Mahon, Sarah McLoughlin, Alison Linney, inspire me every single day as they live with and after cancer. Many, many more inspire me every single day as they live with and after cancer. In my opinion, they are brave - but I'd bet my bottom dollar these women were that way before cancer waltzed into their lives, unwelcome and unexpected. Radio presenter Rachael Bland and campaigner and former teacher Janine Brooke both lived bold and brilliant lives until the very last. But it wasn't the cancer that made them that way. They were those women, regardless of the state of their cells.

I think it's often the way we are perceived to have dealt with the shitty hand we've been given that makes people view cancer survivors (I hate that word) in such an exaggerated way. But here's the thing - what alternative do we have? It's not like we can spontaneously combust because our bodies turn against us. Nor do we have any other choice than to muddle through as best as we can really. In 2018, The Guardian ran an article off the back of some research by Macmillan Cancer Support that explored the idea that "pressure to stay positive may be a negative for cancer patients". Around the time the piece was released, I spoke to a lot of people who had experienced cancer for a piece I was working on with Maggie's Centres covering the language used around cancer. The constant need to be "positive" and the assignment of the "brave" and "inspiring" roles adds unnecessary pressure to patients at a time when they are already facing more pressure then they know what to do with. To paraphrase Bonnie Tyler, at the time I was in treatment (and, some who know me well would probably argue, now) I was living in a powder keg and giving off sparks. I was scared and I was vulnerable and I was exhausted – but whenever anyone asked me how I was doing, I slapped a big smile on my face and told everyone I was "doing fine – all things considered". My mum has always said "fine" means "fucked off, insecure, nervous and exhausted" which at that time I think was totally accurate. Actually, I think that definition is often appropriate. These phrases - positive, brave, inspirational - while well-meaning, restrict cancer patients from feeling able to explore the full range of their emotions frankly and openly. Because to feel fully what they are experiencing may include being negative or feeling sad or low or anxious - and voicing those emotions and fears breaks the facade of representing how they "should" be and "should" feel.

Cancer treatment and beyond has brought out the very best and the very worst of my emotions. It has become increasingly important for me to acknowledge all of the emotions the experience brought, the good, the bad and the downright distressing. I triedx to take note of the days when there weren't many jokes to find, no matter how much I looked like Uncle Fester, regardless of the fact that I described cancer as "a bit of an inconvenience", but my depression has made this more difficult than I'd care to admit. As I'm sure you can imagine, or as you've experienced yourself, there are days when actually, being treated for cancer is pretty shitty. There are times when all you want to do is go for a swim because that's the place you find your clarity but you can't because cancer has taken that away from you. When having to plan for the possibility of kids in your future feels like an alien concept because you don't even know what you want for dinner, can't even plan next week, let alone what you might want to do with your uterus in the future. When you're three weeks post surgery and a couple of slow hours walking around Kew Gardens really knocks you out for the rest of the week. When your wound just isn't healing quite as you'd like. When you're scared about facing chemo and all the unknowns that entails. When you're getting to know an implant that has replaced a huge part of the feminine identity you've had for 26 years (and been hard on for 26 years). When you're trying to prepare yourself for losing your hair against your will. When you're trying to be determined and upbeat but while you're lacking a plan you just feel a bit lost and vulnerable. When you want to be your best – your most positive and healthy and happy self – for the people who love you and spend their time coming to visit you. Those days do happen. And they're hard.

With depression, days on treatment - and those beyond - took on a whole other layer of complexity. It's important to stress here that I do not believe I struggled with my cancer experience more than anyone else may have struggled with theirs as a result of my pre-existing depression. I suppose you could in fact argue that I was more prepared for the volatility of emotions at such a turbulent time because that's the way I'd lived my adult life, when arguably there wasn't much to be worried about. Anyone who has ever had depression knows that's not the way it works though. There is often no cause and effect for depression - it is just something that is - but before I got diagnosed with cancer my emotions often swung uncontrollably anyway. Depression definitely meant I interacted with the moods produced by cancer more though. Perhaps more is the wrong word. Differently is probably more appropriate. If I was sad, I would beat myself up for being sad. If I felt tearful or afraid I would reprimand myself for not being strong enough or brave enough. Once again we come back to those terms continually piled on cancer patients. I have a tendency to do this even at the best of times and it can result in some fairly deathly flogging of my self-worth and self-esteem. After my treatment I underwent some fairly serious cognitive behavioural therapy that helped me identify patterns in my behaviour - those where I'd wake up and feel scared about the spectre of chemotherapy hanging over me then proceed to ridicule and condemn myself for such selfish and foolish behaviour. With every negative feeling or emotion, the mental self-mutilation followed. I was a failure for crying, a failure for being angry. I was letting everyone down. I was failing at being a good cancer patient. I was lucky enough to be getting treatment, wasn't I? Lucky enough to have found my lump early. Lucky enough that it had only tiptoed into my lymph nodes rather than making a full-force dash for them.

Lucky. That word comes up again and again for those who survive cancer too. We **are** lucky to be here. We **are** lucky to have brilliant surgeons and medical experts on hand, and our access to them is free. We are **so** lucky in **so** many ways. I am lucky and I strive to remember that every day. But I think that luck can feel like a burden. Because to reward the world for our luck we must be grateful every day, even when our bodies look like war zones and our minds are in the process of scabbing over from the repeated traumas we have experienced. When PTSD is a real issue among those who have lived through cancer. When we may have lost our chances to build a family from scratch as a result of treatment to save our own lives. When families and relationships have been torn down because the stress and the fear become overpowering. Not being grateful enough is something I have consistently given myself grief for, while on the days I may not think straight away about how lucky I am, I have a tendency to berate myself for letting down those who have gone before me. While all of these things are undoubtedly felt by many who have had their own cancer experiences, my ability to run myself ragged with negative self talk is second to none. If negative self talk were an Olympic sport, I would have a cabinet full of gold medals. I'd have enough gold to make even the biggest chrysophilist jealous. (I am adding that word to my vocabulary. It means gold lover. Who knew?! The English language is so rich and full and vibrant and awesome. Alright, alright, I'm sorry. Word nerd over).

There's a big thing about surviving cancer. Everyone who has been there tells you about it but you never believe until faced with it yourself. You can't just go back to how life was before. You will never again be exactly the same person you were before you heard the words "breast cancer" spoken in your direction. There are, obviously, many parts of this which are bloody brilliant. I'm not sure I'll ever work full time again, cos my boob tried to kill me, so I'm exempt from the 9-5 rat race, right? That's what I tell myself when my bank balance is looking a bit on the anaemic side. I'm getting to write this book. I gave up a job I didn't love in favour of a job I do. After being bald, I was forced to try short hair again, loved it and kept it. I have a newfound and deep-seated love and appreciation of the sky. I get to do awesome things with incredible charities. I try not to sweat the small stuff. I have developed brilliant relationships with incredible people. If I didn't feel uncomfortable about using exclamation marks, I'd have included one after every single one of these statements!

But also. Also there are the bad parts. I'm all too familiar with fear. My relationship with my body is being built back up from the ground. I get tired ever so easily. I get palpitations when I go near my hospital. I have nightmares about my breast exploding. Some days I feel inexplicably sad for what I have lost in the last three years. My resilience has been left in tatters. I'm gradually building it back up, brick by brick, but it's slow progress. While I've never felt especially strong or together, things that would once have been, to quote Jinkx Monsoon, "water off a duck's back" in my life before cancer, now stick like tar to feathers. Rebuilding that resilience takes time.

I remember reading an article when I was in the throes of treatment that suggested those who were prone to depression before a cancer diagnosis, like me, were more likely to die of their disease because of their lack of a positive mental attitude. The idea that my positivity, or any lack thereof, could affect my chances of survival was, and remains, a terrifying prospect. At the time of reading the article, it sent me into a tailspin of turmoil. There is a place for a PMA, of course there is. There is absolutely a place for optimism, and there's a place for hope too, but to ask those going through cancer experiences to forgo realism in favour of perpetual positivity is shortsighted and unrealistic, let alone potentially harmful and damaging.

If life during cancer is about covering unchartered emotional territory, life after cancer comes with similar challenges. Life after cancer is a lot about learning how to deal with a whole new tapestry of emotions. "Survival" for want of a better word comes packaged with heavy doses of survivor's guilt, fear of remission, questioning what happened to you, anger that it did, cancer-related loss and grief, the palpable feeling of a metaphorical kick in the gut when someone you know dies, as happens regularly when you've been a resident in Cancerland. After cancer, life becomes about learning how to deal with these things in among all the usual stresses of day to day life. Work stresses mingle with anxiety about an unexplained pain that has been lingering for a few weeks. Before cancer, that pain would probably not have been given a second thought, but after cancer, it's a reminder of the mad old world you live in, where health anxieties can, if not checked, plague your every day. Because it is not beyond the realms of possibility that that pain indicates that the cancer is back and has become incurable. But you can't know until you get those things checked. For me, every niggle, every ache or pain results in a back and forth between my rational brain and my irrational brain (that makes me sound like I have multiple brains like a cow has multiple stomachs, but as far as I know, I do not).

Things that go through my brain when I get an unexplained pain or cough. These things often run through my brain multiple times a day within the space of about 30 seconds of each other: "Am I wasting time if I get it checked and it's nothing? Is it nothing? Am I making it up? Am I making it worse by thinking about it all the time? It's definitely cancer and it has definitely spread but I couldn't possibly have a scan to make sure because that's an awful lot of money for the NHS to spend if it is nothing. It's definitely nothing. Isn't it? Or is it?"

And after cancer, survivor's guilt is real. Real and pervasive. Every time I hear about another person, whether I've met them, kind of half know them or have never heard of them at all, who has been diagnosed with secondary breast cancer or has died from it, I get a little crack in my heart. These cracks deepen the more of this news I hear. I wonder why I was, for now at least, more lucky than them. I wonder why I deserved to survive. I feel an overwhelming sense of responsibility to them to be better, to do more, to make the most of the life that I've been given. I feel guilty for still talking about my experience because at least the active part of treatment is over for me. What about the thousands of other people for whom treatment will never end? They don't want to hear me wanging on about this when I'm lucky enough to have wrapped up my treatment. Life can feel so futile and delicate in the wake of the news that someone else has died because breast cancer chose them. The prospect of continuing on in a life that is so inexplicable, where a disease that you had and appear to have survived is killing other people, can so easily knock you off the post-cancer tightrope "survivors" are striving to balance on a daily basis.

There are people literally fighting for their lives and sometimes I feel like I should sit down and shut up because my opinion of cancer isn't relevant because it's not (currently) trying to kill me. In 2016, I wrote an article for Red about my experience and I got shouted down by a handful of people who thought it wasn't valid and that they should have been telling the stories of people with secondaries instead of me. So often I don't understand why I am still here and so many of my amazing Boobette sisters are not (Boobettes are ambassadors for breast cancer awareness charity CoppaFeel! There are about 120 of us and we are essential the boob chat ninjas of the world who go about the country educating people on the signs and symptoms of breast cancer, encouraging those we meet to check their boobs and empowering them to go to the doctors with any concerns). Honestly, this life after cancer is a bloody minefield – especially if you're prone to excessive rumination like I am.

There is one key thing I have learnt though. I think this lesson has partially occurred as a result of my extensive CBT and counselling but partly just as a result of living through a trauma and probably as I approach 30 and develop a bit of hindsight on the life that has gone before me. The lesson is this: depression or no depression, PTSD or no PTSD, cancer or no cancer, any emotions you are feeling are valid. You're feeling them for a reason. We're all guilty of shutting ourselves down when we're experiencing emotions that feel more intense than we're used to. But they are part of the human experience. They are part of what it is that makes us a human. Without sorrow we cannot know joy. Without loss we cannot know gratitude. I know it sounds trite. I know it sounds a bit airy fairy, a bit wishy washy and probably a bit like I've read too many books on feelings but we are consistently told to keep our emotions in check because we are scared of how our feelings will be perceived. But if your emotions are on extra loud, for whatever reason, sit with them for a while. Don't try to get rid of them. Recognise them. Learn from them. Don't beat yourself up for not reacting the "right" way to something. There is no "right" way. Remind yourself you're doing the best you can. And if the intense emotions you're feeling are horrible or scary, find someone to sit with them with you, someone to hold your hand and remind you that everything's going to be ok. I think every emotion comes to teach us something. We just have to be open to learning.

That's what I'm trying to do every single day. Because this life is tough, man. It's really tough. And adding the extra baggage of unrealistic emotional expectations is only making this life harder.

Right now, to anyone who is feeling an awful lot of feelings, know I'm sending you a squeeze and a gentle, non-patronising pat on the shoulder.

Life is tough, my love, but so are you.

A Friend in Need is a Friend Indeed

I wanted to include a list of ways to look out for a friend or loved one who may be struggling. These suggestions come from my experience of cancer and depression, but I think, I hope, they can be applied for any situation.

1. Feed them. Not every meal. Not every day. But once or twice. If they're struggling with their mental health it's a good way to offer support and remind them they are worthy. If they're going through something like cancer treatment, offering to carry the load of preparing food for them might seem like a small gesture to you, but to them it can be the difference between surviving and crumbling.

2. Go round and do the dishes, run the hoover round or give the place a quick dust. Again. Not every chore. Not every day. But helping your friend sort out their surroundings is another sure fire way to take the pressure off them and one that can have resounding benefits for their mental health, regardless of the issues they're dealing with.

3. Don't just talk about the cancer, or the depression, or the grief, the anxiety or whatever they're contenting with. Remind them that they're a real person of worth and value beyond their current situation by talking about other things too - their interests, your interests, the last book you read, the last film you watched, that funny dog you saw on the internet. Anything to take their mind off their mind or their situation can really help.

4. Don't avoid the difficult topics. Try to remain impassive if

they talk to you about things that might be difficult to hear and prepare yourself for some difficult conversations. Try not to turn to platitudes and remember not to judge them. You could even thank them for being honest with you. And don't hesitate to talk to someone if you need support after these conversations.

5. Take their lead. This one isn't an easy one. Generally I'd say trust your pal and take guidance from them on how they want you to handle the situation. From my experience, those with physical health issues know what they need and want and are just looking for an opportunity to articulate it but this comes with a caveat. Sometimes those who are struggling with mental health issues are resistant to support so you need to step in. Be prepared in these instances to be knocked back but try not to take it personally. Remember it's their illness giving you a hard time, not your friend.

6. Help them seek further support if they need it. If you think they're a risk to themselves or anyone else, don't leave them alone and consider taking them to A&E.

7. Be thoughtful - keep an eye out for things that might hit them hard. Knock backs in life, deaths of friends or loved ones, difficult work situations or familial difficulties can have a huge impact on someone who is already feeling a bit vulnerable. Think about the things that make your life more difficult and recognise that someone who is struggling with their mental or physical health will likely take these things much harder than you expect. React accordingly.

8. Be flexible. Expect cancellations and rescheduling. Your pal probably can't judge how they'll feeling ahead of time

and know that chances are they're beating themselves up if they've had to bail on you. If you had plans to meet somewhere, offer to mix it up a bit and visit them at home or be as accommodating as you can with alternative arrangements.

9. Just be there. You don't actually have to say anything. You don't actually have to do anything. Just going and sitting with them and (if they'll let you) holding their hand can be the biggest gift in the world.

10. Look after yourself as well. There's a phrase I love which is "you can't pour from an empty cup" meaning that you have to be well in yourself to be able to be a good friend to someone who's got shit going on. So make sure that while you're trying to do the best for your friend, you're looking out for number one too.

(Thank you to my brilliant and helpful GP friends for their help with this important list)

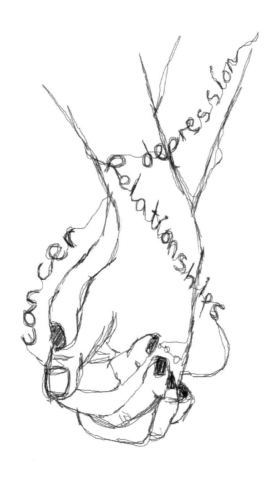

**Chapter 8: Relationships,
Cancer & Depression**

One thing that they definitely don't tell you about being diagnosed with cancer is how to tell the people you love. I have always said that my cancer experience was harder for those around me than it was for me. I know how hard it was for my parents and my sister when their little girl and little sister was going through gruelling treatment to attempt to save her life. But you know, people acknowledge it'll be hard for them. The sentence "my daughter/sister/long term life partner has cancer" is always going to elicit a reaction. "How terrible for you all!" "And she's only 26, how sad!", but how is it for those who say "my friend has breast cancer"? Do people really understand the widespread impact a cancer diagnosis has on those that aren't in the familial inner sanctum? Is it the sort of thing that is just brushed off after a moment or two, while the person who has spoken those words is living with the fear that something terrible might happen to their friend? I don't know - I've never been on that side of things. I've only ever been on the side of breaking the bad news about myself. And I can tell you it is one of the strangest experiences I've ever had.

Telling my family was hard (though that doesn't seem like a big enough word) but there was one friend in particular who I was anxious about telling. When it dawned on me I had to break this news to her, I knew how it would affect her, and that was more upsetting to me than the tumour growing in my breast. Her family had had its unfair share of cancer and I had known her for most of my life. We had been friends for a very long time and it was as hard to tell her as it was to tell my immediate family. Hers is another face I think I will remember for a long time. I think I'll also remember Chris bringing her a cup of tea and my Mum giving her a hug. "Are you alright?" I asked her. My mum: "She's just feeling exactly how we all felt a few hours ago, Alice. A bit shocked." It seems like we all have a tendency to underplay this.

But again, I was lucky, as with so much of my cancer experience. I had someone to share the load with. Chris and I formulated a list of people we wanted to tell, and we split it, though in truth, he did most of the telling. He left my parents' house for a couple of hours on the day I was diagnosed to tell his family and to break the news to a few of the key people in our lives. I asked him how everyone was. How they took it. If they were going to be OK. Which sounds selfish in a way, right? Why did I think this news would affect them so much? But we have always had a very tight bunch of friends and hearing about their reactions added another layer of realism to the situation. Hearing that one friend was on a night out in Central London and was a bit past his best, read, hammered, (he was one of the few people who knew that I'd had tests and as soon as Chris called him, he knew what the topic of conversation was before Chris had even raised it. I still feel bad about ruining his evening but I'm pretty sure we've made up for it since) felt quite fitting and reminded me that life was carrying on outside of this little cancer bubble I had found myself in. This was something I had to remind myself of often throughout treatment. The list of people we wanted to tell face to face, or as close to as we could manage, formed the basis of the list of people we eventually invited to our wedding. I'm not going to lie, that list made selecting wedding guests mega easy.

And speaking of weddings, I had never wanted to get married. I was always adamant I would never love anyone in a romantic way. I was never a child who planned out every detail of my wedding as I waited patiently for Prince Charming to come and sweep me away. I was fiercely independent, determined that I didn't need a partner to make me happy or whole. I guess I was kind of a lonely kid too. I was pretty weird (hey - I heard you snort, I know I'm still weird but I'm OK with it now), spent a lot of time with my face in a book, reading about magic and adventures and monsters and admirable women. I never read romantic books really. The list of books I have read famously, embarrassingly, misses out many of the classic romances. I was never interested in Mr Darcy nor did Heathcliff set my soul on fire with his steamy looks in the wilds of the moors. I never planned to find love. But I did. And I found it significantly sooner than I had anticipated.

We first met when we were around 15. I was dressed as Bob the Builder. His hair stuck up in a style reminiscent of Simon from The Inbetweeners and he wore oversized ice hockey jerseys of American and Canadian teams he watched on the TV in the early hours of the morning. When I was not dressed as Bob the Builder (perhaps, when I was too) I was a classically awkward teen who preferred to hang out in the library than get pissed on a Saturday night like many of my peers who had discovered alcohol pretty early on. I'd found a space for myself with the local am-dram society where I could sing show tunes at the top of my voice, throw on costumes and pretend to be someone else for a few hours a week. I harboured ambitions of going to theatre school, singing and acting for a living. We were two very different human beings who lived in different towns, but in the age of MSN we kept in touch, seeing each other every couple of months as he lit the stages I was performing on. We kissed for the first time when we were 17, when I was once again wearing a costume - but this time a gorgeous couture dress designed and made by my sister during her time at university. It was based on Titania from A Midsummer Night's Dream. It was a distinctly more appropriate costume for a moment that would change the course of my life forever.

I won't bore you with the early details of our relationship. It was too long ago for it to really mean anything and we were children. I was complex and he was kind. I was too skinny, barely eating and he took me to Burger King and encouraged me to eat. He taught me what it was to love and I still wonder how I was lucky enough to find this guy without having to kiss that many frogs. I went to uni over 100 miles away. We grew separately. We grew together. And I swear this is the reason our relationship has had the longevity it has. We moved in together not far from our respective towns in the North East of England when I finished my degree. We went through stressful job changes, I worked in Durham for three months in a job where I cried every day I was there. He found me sobbing in the shower one morning and told me it wasn't worth it. I quit. I got a job in London, one that I applied for without talking to him about. I asked him if he was coming with me. He said yes. We uprooted our lives and moved from a spacious 2 bedroom, 2 bathroomed flat with a big kitchen and kittens which we paid £460 a month for to a small but perfect for us one bedroom flat in London where the rent was £1000 a month. I was an intern. He started what's now his career. A rumour went round his place of work that he was "only 26" when he started. He was 21.

Our lives seemed to be going well. We moved again. Twice in fact. I was in a stable job. He was in a stable job. We had bought a flat we adored and we were happy. I had my own struggles, as I had done throughout our relationship, but he guided me through them. When depression made the rest of the world feel like it was crumbling around me, he was my steady guide - holding up the walls and clearing a path for me to pick my way through. He carried me when I couldn't carry myself. He made me laugh, every single day.

On the day I was diagnosed with breast cancer, he was with me. I've already talked about his hand on the small of my back, already described the lack of colour in his face after they said the words neither of us had wanted to hear. The words we hadn't really allowed ourselves to imagine we would hear. I said to him, "I know we have been together a long time. But this is going to be hard. It's going to be horrible. I am offering you the chance to walk away. No hard feelings. If you want to walk away, you can."

He looked at me. Looked me straight in the face and said: "Alice. Can you imagine me on Tinder?" I told him that perhaps, with that in mind, he'd better stick with me.

By this time, we had been together for almost ten years. We had been children and teenagers and we had tiptoed into adulthood. I'd had a companion with me for most of my formative years. We had already faced so much together. And as we stood together that day, shellshocked, in planning mode, trying to process what was ahead and manage the shituation (shit situation) of telling everyone who needed to know, it was pretty obvious there was a lot more coming our way.

There's no doubt that he has seen me at both my very best and my absolute worst. No-one has seen the many shades of me that there are in quite the same way as he has, and I think, if we're being honest, no-one saw the full extent of my cancer treatment in quite the same way as he did. He carried me to the toilet when I could barely move after surgery. He made me drink when my nausea was so intense I could hardly hold my head up. He helped me in and out of bed when my legs wouldn't work as they were supposed to. He persuaded me that I had to go to the hospital for chemo when I cried before every round and told him I didn't want to. We had our Dumbledore Deal, the song he sang me when I couldn't bear to get up and brush my "Queen Latifah's". When cancer made the rest of the world feel like it was crumbling around me, he was my steady guide - holding up the walls and clearing a path for me to pick my way through. He carried me when I couldn't carry myself. He made me laugh, every single day.

But our relationship, despite its strength, wasn't left unaffected by my cancer diagnosis. For a long time, he was my carer, not my partner, or my lover. He was still my best friend, but I saw the toll that my treatment took on him. I watched him as he struggled to deal with what we were facing but strapped on the bravest face he could muster so that I didn't have to see how hard he was finding it. I saw as he panic napped for hours at a time when being conscious just became too much. I heard about when he comfort ate a whole Chocolate Orange in one sitting. Take that, Terry.

Everyone always says how lucky I am to have found someone so remarkable when I was so young. And I am lucky. I am grateful pretty much every day (unless he snoozes his alarm for TWO WHOLE HOURS which he has been known to do). But while we are lucky, we have worked hard. We work hard every day to be thankful for each other. We have worked hard to let each other know how much we mean to one another. If I ask him how much he loves me (and I do, often, because that's another thing about depression - it makes you question every relationship in your life on practically a daily basis), he'll simply raise his right hand, thumb facing towards him, little finger facing towards me. From the palm of his hand, right round the world and to the back of his hand. "From here, right the way round the world and back to here". He works hard to live with me, because I am not the easiest to live with. I work hard to live with him, because I am not the easiest to live with. And we have had to work hard to rebuild our relationship from that of patient and carer to something more like that of any other married couple. We've had to try and re-level the playing field. And as I've had surgery after surgery to repair my breast, self esteem and body confidence (just those tiny things) it's been practically impossible to establish an even keel between ourselves for any length of time. We have worked hard. And we continue to work hard.

There is no-one that a cancer diagnosis leaves untouched. Friends, family and colleagues all feel the aftershocks of someone telling them they have cancer. But I think I included this chapter because, more than anything, I wanted to write about love. I wanted to write about love in all the forms and shapes and styles and colours and textures it comes in. While I might try to pretend otherwise, I am a hopeless romantic. Not for the kind of love you read about in fairytales or see unfold on Hollywood screens, but for the quiet love that presents itself in the unexpected ways. I wanted to write about the kind of love that is demonstrated by a mother who obsessively cleans toilet doorhandles while her daughter is on chemotherapy because she's scared of her getting an infection. The father who sits in the breast clinic, desperately uncomfortable, but determined to be there for his daughter. The love of a friend who sits in a hospital waiting room and manages to make a patient laugh themselves to the verge of tears because, even though they're terrified, they know they're loved. It's the love of a friend who has to take a step back because they can't cope with seeing someone they care about going through hell. The text messages that aren't about cancer. The ones that ask how you are and genuinely want to know. It's a shift in the relationship between siblings that goes from perfunctory and irregular communication to the essential and frequent and the daily exchanges of two best friends.

I wrote this for a piece of fiction I was working on a few years ago and it's something I thought about regularly during my cancer treatment, and something I think about a lot beyond that too.

Love is warmth when the boiler is broken. It's lazy Sunday mornings and breakfast in bed. It is brightness when you feel all the lights have gone out. It's the colour in a grey day. It's hope just before the sun sets. Love is a silly dance by way of an apology, a cup of coffee made first thing on a morning, a glass of milk last thing at night.

It's the quiet moments when no-one is looking – the squeeze of a hand. The stroke of a face. It isn't grand gestures, it's not racing heartbeats or extravagant gifts. It's the simple things. The irreplaceable things.

When all else fails, we love. That's what love is.

We require different kinds of love at different times in our lives but humans fundamentally need love to function. We are not designed to fly solo. To offer up a quote from 90's silver screen star Hugh Grant (jokes, this is obviously from the infinitely more "literary" and "high brow" John Donne), "no man is an island". Or to paraphrase an old African proverb, living life takes a village of love. But that love doesn't always come easily. It is not easy to love someone who is going through cancer treatment, nor is it easy to love a person who has depression.

And relationships do suffer through both of these things. As with every single facet of life, there are highs and there are lows but it's about riding the storm together, I guess. My relationship with my husband has gone from strength to strength as a result of my cancer treatment. My friends have been incredible. People I knew would step up have stepped up in ways beyond that which I ever could have imagined - coming to hospital appointments with me, seeing significantly more of my body than I ever anticipated they would, letting me cry when I needed to, being my cheerleaders and my personal trainer, my confidantes and my personal chefs. All of the relationships I had already established before I got sick have gone through their own form of evolution. Some have faded, some have strengthened. Some people have taken on a new role within my life. I have taken on new roles within others' lives. Everything and nothing has changed in the same breath.

Through the last three years I have found myself alongside a horde of people I never would have anticipated meeting. I have forged many new relationships as a result of cancer. In fact, pretty much all of the relationships I have forged over the last few years have come as a result of cancer. I meet so many people now, but more often than not, these are people who have experienced cancer, or have loved someone who has. These days, I work alone. I spend my working week tapping away at a computer, some days not seeing or talking to anyone until Chris gets home from work. So I meet fewer people that way. But I meet a lot of people who have been on the receiving end of the cancer news. And by God am I glad about that. I wish none of them had had cancer, but I'm glad that it's the shared experience which has brought these people into my life.

Those who have experienced cancer become a kind of tribe. Regardless of age, gender or whether you've had breast or ovarian cancer, lymphoma or Ewing's Sarcoma, we are kind of all in it together and we feel every loss very, very keenly. I know too many people who have died as a result of this disease. In late 2016 when we lost one of our fellow Boobettes, Alex who was just 26, I was devastated. I had never met her, we followed each other on Twitter, but our paths had never crossed in real life. That didn't matter though. We were both Boobettes. She was one of us. One of our own. Her loss was a brutal reminder of why CoppaFeel! has to exist. Another online friend, Dean, died as a result of his Ewings Sarcoma and I was gutted. A longtime friend of my

Mum's, Julie, who had been so kind to me when she found out I was sick and throughout my treatment, died while I was in the process of writing this book. She pledged towards the first print run in my Kickstarter. Her name is in the patrons list but cancer took her before I finished writing. The Breast Cancer Care Fashion Show in 2016 was one of the very best things to come out of me getting this rotten disease, but two of the women who walked alongside me, Janine and Emma, both died as a result of secondary breast cancer in the two years following the show. CoppaFeel! stalwart and fundraising superstar Laura Weatherall-Plane, who I didn't meet, but again knew of, died and left a massive hole behind her too. Radio presenter Rachael Bland changed the conversation around cancer with her podcast You, Me and the Big C, alongside fellow cancer patients Lauren Mahon and Deborah James, but died in 2018, leaving a massive legacy behind her. Living in this world, the world where cancer chose to come into my life too and a world where people are still dying because of mutated cells in their body, is not an easy place to be.

And there's the fear that comes with the loss of every person you know or "know". And the guilt. The fear because you can't guarantee that the same won't happen to you at some point in the future. The guilt for even thinking about it when you should be thinking about the person who has died rather than thinking about yourself. And the guilt that if you've made it through the thing that so cruelly killed them, you should be doing a lot more with your life. You should be doing it for them and every other person who has been killed by this disease that you have somehow escaped, rather than finding yourself sobbing in the shower, again, for the fourth time in a week, because cancer happened to you too.

And then I find myself thinking about the other people I've met who have had or are currently living with cancer. I worry for their futures more than my own, truth be told, especially those closest to me. And while the risks of losing these people are almost tangible, not surrounding yourself with these people for fear of loss would be foolish. Because they are your tribe. Because you can learn from them. And if it weren't for cancer you never would have met them. I never feel better about the life that I am creating than when I am surrounded by the incredible life force of the CoppaFeel! Boobettes - an army of women who are dedicating their time to stamping out the late detection of breast cancer, many of whom have had their own experiences of battling with a boob that tried to kill them. It's not very often we're able to get all of these women in one place at one time (there are 115 of us spread across the country from Aberdeen to Plymouth so definitely not easy to organise) but spending any amount of time with these megababes or any of my CoppaFeel! fam, I feel like, perhaps, this whole cancer thing was almost worth it. Because maybe, at long last, I've found my place in the world.

Relationships go through a whole other set of challenges when there are mental health issues involved. I am all too guilty of backing out of events last minute because I don't have the capacity to socialise and I know this comes with a limit. There are only so many times someone can tolerate being backed out on. And I know that there are many times when I am not a good friend - not out of choice but out of the lack of capability. While I don't wholly agree with RuPaul's "if you can't love yourself, how in the hell are you gonna love somebody else?" (there will be people reading this who GASP in horror) I know that when I'm in periods of darkness and can barely look after myself, looking after others and being a good friend, wife, daughter, sister is borderline impossible, making RuPaul's tagline ring true. But I work hard to be all of those things when I have the capacity, despite my distinct lack of self-love, sometimes to my detriment.

I also know that I'm rarely honest about what's going on and one of the things about my depression is that often I can't see that it is happening, only recognising that I've hit the bottom when I've done the legwork to start getting outta there. I've been more honest about my experiences of depression on Instagram than I am with many of the people closest to me. Perhaps the cynics amongst us would say that this is some kind of warped drive for the dopamine-inducing hit of a "like" or a comment, but in reality, it's easier to type some words and send them out into the ether than it is to sit in front of a human who could be personally affected by the things I'm saying, watching their reaction. How can I tell the people who love me the most that I don't feel worthy of the affection they are kind enough to provide me with, that my brain makes me doubt that they really do care about me and that I have thought about ending my tailspin of negative thoughts in the most final way possible?

Relationships go through challenges every single day but I think one of the most important things to remember is that most of the people who love you are invested. They are all in. So while cancer and mental health problems or other issues that we are exposed to on a daily basis might mean that some relationships fail, the ones that don't are the ones that really matter. If your relationships can get through a cancer diagnosis and all the hellish treatment it entails or survive managing a mental health issue that leaves you volatile, it's pretty certain that the person who loves you, loves you regardless of these things, not in spite of them.

I know I have been lucky in pretty much every respect when it comes to the people I have in my life. They've put up with a lot of shit from me and still make an effort to hang around (for reasons which remain mostly unclear to me - perhaps they are gluttons for punishment) and my gratitude for that is totally and utterly endless. Not everyone is that lucky. I know relationships can and do break down when they're put under strain. I'm not trying to deny the strain that cancer and depression inflict on those around you, nor am I trying to berate those that aren't able to stick around and weather the storm. Sometimes people need to escape the rain and the thunder for their own protection - and that's OK too, you know. For all the people who leave, there are people who stay, remaining steadfast, hanging on, taking the trauma on the chin and those people are ready to emotionally bankroll you at a moment's notice. You just need to ask them.

It's taken me a while to articulate these thoughts, because I know my experience is not the same as many others and I want to get it right. I know cancer can devastate relationships as well as create them. But I saw a quote this morning, from an unknown source that seemed to hit the nail on the head when it comes to managing relationships in the depths of, or in the wake of, experiencing a trauma. Regardless of the outcomes or the changes in relationship statuses (in the old fashioned sense of the word, not in the "Facebook official" sense of the word) your illness or the difficulties you are facing do not mean you are a burden: "You are not a burden. You HAVE a burden, which by definition, is too heavy to carry on your own," and while there might be some people in your life who won't pick up the slack, there are lots that will.

Sometimes you've just got to ask.

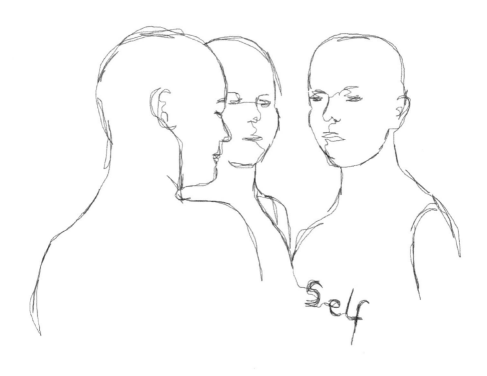

Chapter 9: Self

How many times have you looked in the mirror and criticised what you see before you? How often are the first things you think about the way you look negative? If I'm honest, my answer for most of my life has nearly always been "every day". But I am trying to change that as I grow older and look back on everything my body has been through with gratitude and fondness, rather than constantly berating it for changing and growing and shrinking and not being "perfect".

I stopped eating because I thought I was fat for the first time when I was about four. It was before I had even started primary school that I had deemed myself as not worthy of sustenance because of the size of my body. By the time I hit secondary school at the age of 11, I think every person I knew had gathered up an arsenal of things that they didn't like about themselves. I was no exception. And that was before things with the internet and social media really got going. We just picked stuff up from tv, magazines and advertising, rather than being fed the relentless stream of edited images and unrealistic expectations that young people are subjected to via their mobile phones now. Societal pressures to look a certain way are much harder to avoid than they were when I was younger - and this is having an impact - not just on young people today, but everyone. There is no escape from what the world views as perfect when it's constantly presented to you every time you look at your phone.

My relationship with myself has always been my most volatile one. I think pretty much every woman in the world can say the same. Self confidence is something I've often grappled with. Like most people these days, I scroll through Instagram, Facebook, the Internet as a whole and I'm subjected to images of photoshopped bodies, made to look smaller, more taut, more toned. Skin is brightened and cleared of blemishes, while the softness of being a woman is hardened by airbrushing. Boobs are made bigger, cleavages made deeper and waists are made smaller. We're told to avoid "muffin tops", to strive for a "thigh gap", deal with your "armpit cleavage" (that's the bit of your body that isn't quite arm and isn't quite boob, in case you aren't au fait with this frankly offensive and ridiculous terminology) and battle the "back bulge". God forbid you have "thunder thighs" which mean you must deal with "chub rub", or less colloquially your thighs touching. We're told to stay alert in case we become the owner of crows feet, orange peel skin, love handles, cankles, burger nips, sag-bags, thighbrows, a bubble butt. Jeez. Is it any wonder we're a) riddled with self doubt and b) bloody exhausted by the societal constructs our bodies are held up against?

We're fed adverts every second breath telling us how to get glossier hair, we're subjected to images that suggest women are little more than a pair of perfectly pert breasts. Or magazine articles that exclaim "Fix your eyebrows, find love!" These articles, adverts, posts, messages all tell us how we "should" look. And they permeate every waking breath of our lives. Have you ever tried counting how many adverts you see on your commute? Have you ever taken note of how many outlines of cookie cutter models you see when you're strolling down the high street? We are spoonfed these images and these ideas on an almost constant basis. Of course we feel bad about ourselves because feeling bad about ourselves has been monetised by capitalism. Creating a world of people who feel bad about themselves is good for business - it sells more mascaras, sells more clothes, makes us think we need to be skinnier. And don't even get me started on the way social media is impacting our mental health and body image. If you're predisposed to being hard on yourself, living in the world we do can be suffocating and overwhelming even when you're at your healthiest and most positive.

These things and the world we're living in mean self-confidence is hard at the best of times. What do you do then, when you find yourself squidgy round the edges because a gruelling healthcare routine has left you with little time or energy to put on your running shoes? When you no longer have any hair at all, let alone hair that you need to make thicker? Or when one of the parts of your body that defines you as a woman is taken away from you? When you haven't a single eyebrow hair to speak of, when you couldn't make your brows "on fleek" if you tried. How do you find self confidence if you don't even recognise the face, the body, looking back at you in the mirror? When you're as far away from how you "should" look, as you possibly can be?

Being proud to say positive things about your face, body, personality and your skills is often frowned upon in our society, so we don't do it. Or we don't feel like we can because we'll never match up the ideals that are imposed upon us. I suppose doing so could be seen as an act of war. Self confidence often gets confused with arrogance, much like its close sibling, self belief. People would far rather pick at things they don't like than look at the things they do like. Striving for self confidence is a battle - even the most body positive people I know struggle from time to time, but Body Positive activist Megan Jayne Crabbe puts it perfectly in her book *Body Positive Power* when she says "We can't see the beauty in everything that we are because we've been taught to first see everything that we're not." Reframing the way your body looks after years of being taught that it's not good enough takes time.

When I was in treatment, I remember stepping out in a swimming costume for the first time in seven months. Chemo and surgery both played a part in stopping me from doing one of my favourite things as my body needed time to heal from being cut open and my immunosuppressed body couldn't deal with any germs that might have been floating around in the water. I didn't wear a hat to cover the duckling fuzz that was starting to grow back on my head, nor did I have my swimming prosthetic, Rebecca Adlington, to hide the fact that I was down to a uniboob. I was terrified. I worried about what people would think of me if they noticed how lopsided my boobs were. Scared that people would judge me and my bald head, my tired eyes and my pasty skin. I was nervous I wouldn't be able to swim fast or for long any more. All of these things came down to my self confidence. And there were two things my friends said to me that gave me pause, and helped me park my insecurities. "No one will notice what you look like because they'll all be too worried about what they look like" and "you may be being treated for cancer, but you're still a swimmer. That hasn't changed."

And when I got in the pool, it didn't matter. I did get some weird looks, but I get weird looks when I'm not bald. And I reminded myself that it was OK to look like a cancer patient. Because that's what I was at the time. It wasn't all I was, but it was a big part. And that was OK. Thinking about that moment in the pool takes my breath away now. It's the perfect reminder of how far I have come, even when I feel like there is still so far to go.

That's not to say I'm any more confident than I was BC (before cancer) but I guess the goalposts have moved or the parameters have changed. Whichever cliche you want to adopt. I made a list of things I decided not to moan about when I didn't have cancer and some of the more superficial of them include "bad hair days" or "looking like shit". I always said if I've got hair, eyelashes, eyebrows and skin that doesn't look like tracing paper, I'm a step ahead of cancer me, but the truth is that cancer leaves behind a war zone of scars and imperfections that it takes time to come to terms with. And even after having the opportunity to see the worst you can possibly look, it doesn't take long for that creeping self-doubt to make its way back into your mental vernacular. I swore I'd never complain about bad hair days - but of course I do. Having cancer hasn't miraculously cured me of all of my body hangups. While I'm grateful to the old thing for carrying me through treatment, it's still far from "perfect". I'm attempting to make my peace with that every day. And I know there are hundreds of thousands, millions probably, of people who are trying to make peace with their own bodies in their own ways too.

For me, it's not just the media that tells me these things either. While I suppose it could be said that the media is still to blame, I live with a quiet voice in my head that regularly tells me I am worthless. That my body is the wrong shape and the wrong size. That I need to do more exercise and that I'm stupid for putting that cake into my mouth. That my partner will never find me attractive again because of the scars my body is riddled with. Depression plays a massive part in the way that I view my self. As much as I am hyper-critical of my every behaviour, every thought, every decision, I am critical of every part of my body. This criticism is yet another part of the relationship I have with myself that results in suffocating and negative self talk that borders on verbal abuse. It is toxic. Even when I was in the throes of cancer treatment and unable to drag myself to the toilet without a great deal of buildup, I still chastised myself for not doing enough exercise. For putting on too much weight. For comfort eating. While I know that this is natural for many, it's not a healthy way for us to perceive ourselves. My body is so changed from my cancer treatment, covered in scars and altered in shape and size, but how could it not be? And to berate myself for that is cruel and callous. But that's what depression is. It is the cruel voice inside your mind that kicks you when you're down.

Getting used to the scars I have has been a big part of rebuilding and reconnecting with my self confidence. Scars are so often perceived as imperfections. They're seen as ugly, something we must strive to feel confident "in spite of", rather than "with". I've always been pretty accident prone. When I was a kid, I was forever falling over, walking into things and falling off things. As a result, I'm covered in little scars. Tiny little white flecks across my body that remind me of a place and time in my life. When I look at my knees (which admittedly, I don't do often because that would be weird) I can see the scar from the day I fell off the wall at school. I remember the thick scab that covered the wound as my skin fused together again. When I look in my face in the mirror, I see the single thin line from my forehead to my chin, an outline of the story where I dragged the cat down the stairs by her tail and got my comeuppance for it.

As I grew older, I got a few scars too. My TB jab, reminding me of the secondary school I hated and the bullies who threatened to punch it. I have a scar on my left breast from where the fibroadenoma I had a few years ago was removed. I learned while I was bald that I've got two tiny scars on the back of my head. And there are other marks too. And all of them link together in a tapestry of history, a timeline of events where my body has suffered some kind of trauma and recovered itself. I've always been proud of these scars. Every time I bash myself on the doorway as I rush from A to B, I like it when a bruise blooms underneath my skin, a mark of a moment. It makes a story to tell. And I deal in stories. But the scars I got in my childhood don't impact my self-confidence in the way the scars from my cancer experience do.

Now I have a whole range of new scars, new tales to relay. From where they inserted a PICC line in my left bicep that travelled straight to my heart so drugs could be administered easily and blood could be removed without stabbing around for a vein. Come to think of it, there's also my thick, rigid vein, damaged by the drugs – admittedly not a scar per se, but an external reminder of internal healing. The tiny pinpricks on my stomach from injection after injection to rebuild my immune system after every battering it took from chemo. The three tiny little tattoos to mark where they blasted me for radiotherapy. The slash across my chest where they took out the cancer, and eventually my breast tissue, leaving behind an envelope of skin, a stark reminder of what the last three years have been about – as if I needed one. The scar that circles my left nipple and makes it's way below the cup of my breast and works its way around the underside of my boob after the mastopexy which aimed to make my real breast and my fake breast symmetrical. The pockmarks at the crease of my groin which indicates where I was liposuctioned for my reconstruction.

But these scars are different. Part of me wishes I could leave them behind, that they didn't exist so I wouldn't have to carry them with me forever. So that when this chapter of my life is done, I can move on and forget about it. But that's just fantasy. There are many more scars – those that aren't physical that I'll carry with me, so even if there were no scars casting patterns across my skin, there'd still be those to contend with. I've always marvelled at the scars I got before I had breast cancer. I've always been proud and fascinated by my body's ability to heal and regenerate.

I guess the scars I have from getting breast cancer weren't caused by my own clumsiness. I didn't walk into cancer. Didn't fall over it because I wasn't paying attention. These scars happened because my body turned against me. Because my breast tried to kill me. That's something that I have to come to terms with, just one of the mental cuts I have to allow to heal. At the same time though, they tell a story too. That same story of regeneration and healing as all my other scars, just on a larger scale. They show a strength I never knew I had. A resilience I never imagined I'd be able to find. So I guess I should be proud of them. And proud of everything they represent. I guess I just have to give my mind time to scab over and heal before I can accept the physical traces of cancer. And how my body has changed and continues to change in the aftermath. Perhaps, in fact, seeing my body change so dramatically will help me quiet the aggressive voice that tells me it is worthless. Because I know now it is not. It may have tried to kill me, but it made me survive cancer too. And I should strive to remember that. To make the voice that tells me that I survived overpower the other guy. The crappy, negative voice is such a party pooper.

So how do we make good with our bodies? How do those who have survived cancer come to terms with the body that has been left behind? How do those who experience anxiety and depression teach themselves that they are enough, they will never be "too much"? I know that in amongst all of these bitter and berating thoughts, I am incredibly privileged as a white, straight, cis-gender woman. I'm privileged because even if I criticise my body, internally and externally, I'm still fairly at home there and I don't live with the struggles of others in a less privileged position. But we know that crippling self-doubt when it comes to body confidence is epidemic. It covers all races, all genders, all ages, all orientations. But rather than thinking about what our body should look like, I'm trying to reframe my ideas into what my body does, regardless of it's size and shape. I am grateful for this body that jiggles and wriggles while I dance completely freely. I am grateful for these lungs that allow me to fill up and expand every single day, for the heart that pumps the blood around my body, for these fingertips that can feel the warmth of living and for the tastebuds that allow me to experience life beyond what I see in front of me. I am grateful for everything that makes me human. I am grateful for everything that makes me human, warts and all.

In 2015, artist Caroline Caldwell shared a piece of her work alongside the quote: "In a society that profits from your self doubt, liking yourself is a rebellious act". This couldn't be more true. I'm tired of letting my brain tell me my body is worthless when it does all of these wonderful things on a daily basis so when I criticise myself for having "bingo wings", I've begun asking myself why I think that. What has made me feel like the shape of my arms is not correct? When I tell myself I need to lose some weight, I've begun asking who I "need" to lose weight for. Unless the answer is "for yourself", I'm no longer interested. Mostly.

Next time you're brushing your teeth or your hair, or figuring out if you really can wear that skirt with that top (by my rules, you definitely can, I know I can't see, but you can), I'd like you to do something for me. Look at yourself. Really look and find one thing you love about yourself. Maybe you've got beautiful eyes, maybe you've got really full lips, maybe your cute button nose is a real family trait. Perhaps you can look at your body and be proud of the strength you see in your biceps or calves or maybe you've got stretch marks that prove you're a Mama and you love them because they show you carried another human for 9 months.

We give ourselves such a hard time over our bodies. Even people who seem super confident and like beacons of self love almost certainly have some kind of hangups. But, as the old adage goes, it wouldn't do if we were all the same.

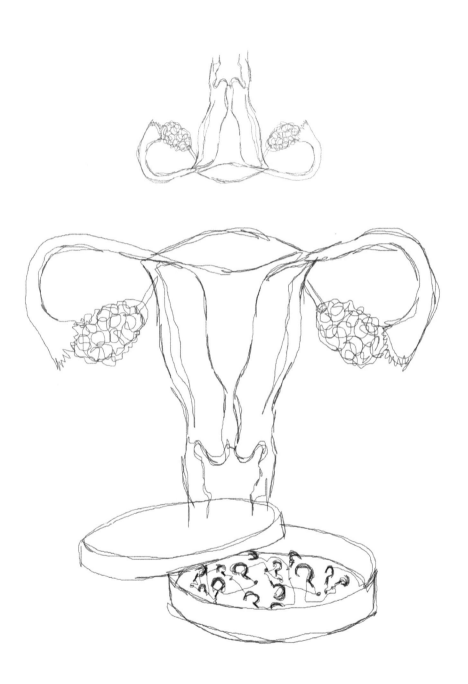

Chapter 10: (In)fertility

Much like I've never considered myself the marrying kind, I've never considered myself the maternal kind either. I've never harboured the deep-seated, biological urge to procreate that women are expected to have. I've been told time and time again that I'll probably change my mind, that when I get older I'll reconsider, but as of yet, there's zero sign of that happening. I'd never say never, but for me the prospect of growing a human from scratch fills me with dread. The idea that something would be relying on me to grow and develop, that I should be responsible to nourish and provide for it gives me an overwhelming feeling of anxiety, and I know a thing or two about anxiety. I've seen so many strong women crippled by fear (not to mention nausea and exhaustion) as a result of pregnancy. Women much more steady with themselves than I am are spending months at a time on the edge of some kind of nervous breakdown because they're shouldering the responsibility for housing a human until it's ready to come out into the world. I just can't imagine being able to face that kind of responsibility and uncertainty without losing what's left of my mind. I genuinely think that mothers are superheroes and I don't bloody know how they do it. (Not to diminish dads here, they're pretty awesome too, but to me, looking at this from the point of view of a woman who is "child-rearing age", growing a human seems fairly incredible.

As a result of these feelings, I'd never considered whether I would be able to have a baby. There's a long running joke that all the women in our family need is to be looked at in the right way to fall pregnant. This is not something I've ever wanted to put to the test so I've always been hyper vigilant when it comes to contraception. But cancer made me confront my fertility, my future plans, and my pre-determined ideals about having a baby in a way I'd never had to before. The thing is, that while trying to save you, chemotherapy has a nasty habit of ravaging your reproductive system, sending you into early menopause. If you don't take action before undergoing treatment, there's a strong chance you'll end up infertile and unable to have children naturally. As a result, many NHS trusts (but unfortunately not all yet) offer the chance for young people going through cancer treatment the opportunity to undergo IVF, but it's not something that's available to everyone. If your cancer is particularly responsive to hormones or especially aggressive, there can be issues with pumping your body full of the tools needed for IVF, or speed may be of the essence. It's a particular problem for younger people who are diagnosed with cancer. Sometimes it's not offered, sometimes the risks aren't made clear, sometimes the system is problematic. My friend Dean, who was diagnosed with Ewings Sarcoma and passed away aged 21, was told that his partner would not be allowed to use his sample after his death because of his sexuality, an issue not afforded to straight couples. But it's so important for young people to protect this facet of their lives, when so many other things are out of control. Campaigner Becki McGuinness was left infertile by cancer treatment in her twenties, after not being told there were any options to preserve her chances of having a baby in the future. Now 30 (at the time of writing), Becki is striving to prevent any other women from having to face the same issues she has. Having babies has never really been on my agenda. I cannot imagine the torture of being a young person who really wants to have kids, experiences cancer and is faced with the possibility that they might not be able to conceive. That prospect must feel so incredibly cruel.

As with most parts of my cancer treatment, I was lucky. Within days of being diagnosed, I found myself sat in the IVF clinic at Guy's Hospital, surrounded by couples who were waiting to find out the status of the little eggs in a Mum-to-be's womb, or finding out if they would ever be able to conceive. I felt like an outsider, like some kind of voyeur looking in on this weird place where dreams were literally coming true or being ripped to shreds with the words "infertile" or "unsuccessful". And I felt like I had found my way there accidentally. I wasn't hopefully pinning my lifelong ambition of having a baby on this incredible procedure. I hadn't tried and failed and felt that heartbreak that the couples around me had endured. I was just there because I'd been told that the treatment that was going to save my life might damage my ovaries. I say just - I know it was a big deal, but I felt like such an imposter,

I've always said that there is no part of your life which is left unaffected by cancer, and this never feels more pertinent to me than when I think about being catapulted into the world of fertility preservation. Against my will I was being told to consider a future I didn't know if I wanted, I didn't know if I would live to see because of those bloody mutated cells causing uproar in my breast. I was furious. As a person who likes to make their own decisions, I felt so frustrated at the idea that such an enormous decision was potentially being taken out of my hands. Because that's the thing about cancer, it forces you to make decisions you've never wanted to make. It forces you to consider things you've never even dreamed of.

Even though I felt confident that I would never want kids, the voices of all those people who had told me throughout my life that I would *definitely* change my mind in the future rang through my brain. It just seemed stupid not to take steps to protect my future self from the heartache of infertility if there was a chance that I might want to make babies in the future. And it wasn't just me either, opting to undergo fertility treatment meant I was protecting Chris from a future where we might not be able to have kids if that was what we decided. But I was 26, facing a long haul of treatment and thinking about the future in such an acute way felt almost suffocating. I was able to definitively decide I wanted a mastectomy, but wasn't able to decide what to have for lunch. I didn't have the capacity to make an informed decision, so I just said yes and began the process of creating, harvesting and storing eggs.

Anyone who has ever had IVF will know what an ordeal it is. For two weeks, I injected myself with hormones which created follicles in my ovaries and turned me into a weepy, snotty, angry mess. The first day I jabbed myself, I cried. I wasn't crying because the injection was painful (though it did sting), I cried because I felt like everything was so out of my control. Jabbing myself with a needle was a reminder that I was in a situation that I had not chosen to be in. A situation I was terrified of, that I was so uncertain of. Being forced to face the fact that I may be unable to conceive a child naturally after attempting to preserve my own life felt like a slap in the face. Salt in the wounds. Pick a simile. Taking out an insurance policy for having a family when I'd never felt like that was something I would want set my teeth on edge. Blame it on my stubborn streak but being forced into planning for something and potentially having the ability to do such a massive thing on my own terms taken away from me, really wound me up. Let's not even discuss the fact that I spent 45 minutes with three women staring up my fanny trying to get my coil out before I even BEGAN the fertility treatment. But after two weeks of injections, more internal scans than I'd care to remember (balk), Chris making his own deposit (not a financial one as I had to clarify to my Mum, nor a refundable one, thank goodness), and an egg harvest under the influence of some bad-man drugs that made my face tingle, the fertility team retrieved 14 eggs, 6 of which were fertilised to create little embryos. Both the eggs and the embryos have been sitting in a freezer at Guy's Hospital since September 2015. Fertility ice pops if you will.

I know tens of thousands of people rely on IVF treatment to grow their families, and I know often these people have to spend a lot of money on doing so. I know that undergoing IVF treatment can be a heartbreaking and difficult journey for families for whom it doesn't work and I appreciate that I haven't had to experience this side of the journey

When a friend of mine asked me what it was like to go through the first stage of IVF treatment, I told her I couldn't remember. To me, it was a supplementary part of my cancer treatment - it wasn't part of the procedure to save my life so I had little to no interest in it. Not only that, but because I wasn't, and never had been, craving kids, it seemed more like a "desirable" than an "essential" part of my treatment, and thus, I probably didn't give it the gravitas it deserved. I guess you could say I was somewhat preoccupied.

But while I made this decision to take out a baby insurance policy and while I've never really felt any of those maternal urges, there's something bigger at play in my reticence to have kids, I think. There's a belief that depression, or a tendency towards it, is hereditary and I find this incredibly difficult to get past. As a result, I've always been wary of passing on my idiosyncrasies (to put it nicely) to any child of mine. My concerns about creating, carrying, birthing and caring for a child are manyfold but there are two things that really strike me when I consider having kids. First of all, I'd be worried about how being pregnant would affect my already volatile mental health. During pregnancy, hormone changes can affect brain chemicals and cause depression and anxiety in those who aren't already prone. My fear is that if I'm volatile without those pregnancy chemicals swimming around in my body, what will I be like when my body is undergoing all of the changes that come with pregnancy? I'm scared of the prospect of my already out of control hormones becoming yet more uncontrollable. I know it's uncharacteristic (ha ha hahahaha) but I also worry about what kind of parent I would be. If you ignore the cancer part, I live a pretty charmed life. I have a brilliant husband who would make an exceptional father. I have a roof over my head. I have a supportive family. But I'm not exactly the most stable of people without the additional stress of a crying, shitting, vomiting, incommunicative being who relies on me to survive. Look how I just described that baby too. Those are not the sort of words used by someone blessed with the mothering instinct, amirite?

While I know many of them would argue otherwise, and while I know that not all mothers are the same, I see those in my life as anchors. People who are steady and able to withstand any storm that comes their way. They are oak trees who may lose branches or may creak in the wind. But they do not fall. In comparison, I feel like a newly grown tree. If silver maples are in fact weak, brittle trees that crack and break, unable to weather the storm (as my research - a simple Google - suggests), I am significantly more like that silver maple than an oak. Let's not even get into the treacherous territory of post-natal depression that I feel I would not be able to survive. Perhaps this strength is something that comes with time. Perhaps this is something which is forced upon you when you become a parent, borne out of necessity. If you are going to be a parent you must be stronger than Superman, braver than Merida and smarter than Steven Hawking. Perhaps the process of becoming a mother is a byproduct of those bloody pregnancy hormones that wreak such havoc on women everywhere. Perhaps it's just something those mothers do, because it's what they have to do. They have no choice. But I feel like my mental health and the variable state of it forces me to make a choice.

And the irony of the fact that worries about my depression and anxiety may stop me from having kids is not lost on me. Perhaps if I was programmed with that maternal vibe it's something I could get past. Perhaps if I had more maternal inclinations I'd be able to ignore the voice in my head that tells me that my mental health combined with pregnancy hormones is like pulling the pin on a hand grenade and waiting for it to explode. Throw in the fact that there's a strong chance any children I do have will have an increased risk of breast cancer as a result of their genetics - I just wouldn't want them to live in a world where they might have to experience the things that I have, from the fights with my brain to the chemotherapy that I needed to save my life.

I know also, that this is all just pure speculation. That I cannot know how my brain and body will react to bringing a baby into the world. I know that, possibly, probably, stopping myself from having kids on a "what if" could be foolish. But my overactive brain cannot help but see and anticipate the worst in any given situation. And as I sit here, nearly three years out from my breast cancer diagnosis, with the age of 30 edging ever closer, I wonder about this "older" that people talk about when they tell me I'll almost certainly change my mind about my decision. People don't tell me that I'll like tea and coffee when I'm older, so why are they so convinced that I'll want to procreate?

Sometimes, like when I spend time with my nephew, I wonder about the sort of mother I would be. I play with him and our imaginations set each other's on fire. I enjoy hanging out with him and chatting to him and teaching him - but I know that there is little risk of him acquiring my idiosyncrasies. I'm not BRCA positive, neither is my sister, so the chances of him being affected by breast cancer are no more likely than any other Tom, Dick or Harry either. He's protected by acquiring my sister's genetics, rather than whatever messed up code decided to give me cancer at 26.

He plays into my thoughts a lot too when I think about having kids. He turned four the day my mum shaved my head. He was scared by the bald and sickly looking woman standing in front of him. He didn't recognise his Auntie Alice as the person he knew. Shortly after my fourth or fifth chemotherapy session, I was at home for Christmas and he was anxious, nervous, unsettled by how careful he had to be around me. It breaks my heart a little bit to know there was a Christmas in his life when he had to worry about what was going on with me. If I had a choice, I would never have wanted that for him. With my own children I have a choice. I've talked before about the likelihood of cancer making a reappearance in my life. Even if I don't have a recurrence of this cancer, I'm still only going to be 36 when I hit 10 years clear. There's practically another lifetime in which I could get cancer again after that. If I've built a life after cancer including little lives, I don't want them to go through what my little nephew went through.

I am by no means saying that women who have had cancer shouldn't have kids. As far as I'm concerned, that is as absurd as saying women who have kids shouldn't be war correspondents or police officers or in the army. Women should have the choice to do whatever they want with their lives, babies or no babies. I do not speak for all women and I never will, but I think the combination of cancer and mental health problems in *my* life mean I am a candidate who should seriously consider their suitability to create a family. So I do. It's not a decision I think should be taken lightly.

And I get frustrated by the idea that as a woman, my role in the world is to reproduce. I was in the oncology ward one day with my Mum as I waited for an appointment to check my bloods and symptoms ahead of my next round of chemotherapy when a woman asked Mum if it was her or me who was in for treatment. When Mum told her it was I who had breast cancer, the woman responded "She'll be ok. She's young. And she'll still have her other breast to feed her babies." If you're sensitive to language, I suggest you skip to the next sentence because WHAT THE ACTUAL FUCK? While I appreciate this comment came from a good place, it suggested that I should be more concerned about my ability to feed a baby than whether or not I was going to lose my breast, or die from the cancer that was trying to kill me. There is so much pressure on women to be mothers, I think part of my resistance comes back, once again, to my stubborn nature. I don't want to do something just because everyone tells me I should want to. I only want to do things, especially of this magnitude, that I want to do. But so often that's presented as a negative and selfish trait. In an overly populated world, I'd argue it's actually the opposite. Who am I to say that but a childless egotist, right?

I do worry (ha, that's new isn't it?) that if I'm not a mother, what else can I be? In this world beyond cancer, I am constantly trying to find out who I am and I'm always striving not to be defined by my cancer experience. I'm sure I must have said this before, but if I didn't know who I was before cancer, how can I possibly know who I am now? I have been in a happy and settled relationship for 13 years so I don't need to spend time looking for the love of my life (thank god, pretty sure I'd be the world's most terrible dater). When my own crippling self doubt eases off temporarily and allows me to, I feel relatively stable in my career. I'm consistently working to try to control my mental health and live in a positive way. But it's almost like I've been programmed to think that without a baby attached to my one remaining nipple, which may or may not be fully functional after a mastopexy which was carried out to make my "good boob" look the same as my "bad boob", I'm letting the side down in some way.

I don't know what the answer is here. It's a minefield. But one thing I do know is that I am not sure if I am a) willing or b) able (mentally or physically) to reproduce. And while the "you'll change your mind one day"'s might be said with an open heart and all of the good will in the world, for now, I'm enjoying being able to just shout "OVARY BAN" at anyone who mentions kids to me. Because if the doctor tells you you're on an ovary ban and shouldn't even consider starting a family until you hit five years cancer clear, why wouldn't you use that as an excuse to scare people into minding their own business?

31 Things Not to Say to Someone Going Through Cancer Treatment (or be prepared for the consequences)

1. Have you tried eating more kale?
2. It's not the cancer that kills you, it's the chemotherapy
3. Hey! At least you get a free boob job!
4. My aunt's dad's sister's cat had that and died
5. At least it's the GOOD kind of cancer!
6. You should probably wear a wig, it'll make other people feel better
7. I'm just really struggling with your diagnosis
8. It's so hard to see you in such a mess
9. God, you really do look poorly
10. My cousin's friend's sister's granny cured their terminal cancer with turmeric! TURMERIC!
11. Look on the bright side! Things could be worse!
12. I've always wanted to shave my head - it must be so freeing!
13. Cancer is so much easier than it used to be!
14. There's always someone worse off than you
15. I know exactly how you feel - it's like when I had that cold last week
16. Exercise is the best way to deal with fatigue!
17. OMG, I know exactly what you mean when you say you're tired. I barely slept a wink last night!
18. You are so brave
19. Just absolutely must just keep positive. It's a positive mindset that beats cancer
20. You're so lucky
21. Did you see that [z-list celebrity] lost their battle with cancer? So sad!

22. Wow, you are, like, clean bald aren't you?
23. Carrot juice will 100% stop your cancer from coming back
24. Cancer feeds off sugar. You really shouldn't be eating that cake
25. You just need to get out there more and stop sleeping so much
26. Make sure you're getting plenty of rest!
27. You don't look like you have cancer
28. You should read about this diet I read about online
29. Chemotherapy is a scam created by big pharma companies to make money
30. I know you'll be fine
31. You just had your last radiotherapy/chemo/surgery? Thank God it's all over!

NB: This is a flippant list of examples. Most of the time during my treatment, I acknowledged that most of the things people were saying came from a good place. More often than not, these things were said as platitudes because they didn't know what else to say. So, as a person going through treatment, try not to be too hard on the loved ones who say something thoughtless. I reckon 95% of the time, they just panicked, and didn't think

Chapter 11: Letters to My Body

Dear Body,

Here we are. Age 15. We've been putting up with each other for a
fairly long time. I'm practically an adult now. Everyone told me
that growing up would make me like my body more, but I'm not
going to lie, body, I still do not like you very much. OK, maybe you
get me from A-B and whatever, but do you really have to do it in
quite such a massive way? You're so TALL, taller than most of
the boys in my year and you definitely have man shoulders. And
thunder thighs. And these bloody enormous boobs you've given
me seem excessive, to say the least. My sister has the perfect
feminine frame. She's tall, but not freakishly so, she's got lovely
long limbs and she's gorgeously graceful. Me, on the other hand?
I lollop about, falling over, crashing into things and generally
taking up far too much room. My thighs rub together when I walk
and my hip are massive. I look at people who are built narrowly
and slenderly and wonder what I did wrong to get given this god-
awful figure. I eat too much too. I'm greedy and I put all of the
wrong things in my body. Too much chocolate. Too much cake.
Too much. I am just too much.

Do you remember being one of the first girls in our primary school
to develop breasts? These puffy things emerged from nowhere
overnight. I was pissed off with you then, and even though that
was a few years ago now, I'm still pissed off with you about it. No
warning. And why did they have to appear so early? Why couldn't
you have waited until other people's boobs started growing so I
didn't stick out like a sore thumb. Honestly, getting ready for PE
was an absolute nightmare. Other girls in class whispered about
you behind their hands as my femininity blossomed at my chest
and I began the process of "becoming a woman". That sounds
like such bollocks doesn't it? Surely I began the process of
becoming a woman when I was born with two X chromosomes. It

didn't happen overnight when my hormones decided to make my chest puff up.

I genuinely do not believe any boy will ever find me attractive. How could they? My stomach is made up of fat rolls, my hips, much like my boobs, appear to have blossomed out of nowhere overnight. At first, I tried polo necks to hide my bangers. That quite obviously just made things worse. It was like trying to hide Mount Everest under a napkin – looking all the more stupid because there was a NAPKIN blowing in the wind on the top of the Earth's largest bloody mountain.

I just don't understand why I couldn't just be given a perfect and petite figure. I wouldn't mind being tall if I wasn't so wide as well. It's the hips. And the backside. Big. Bulbous. I look at magazines and I feel sick to the pit of my flabby stomach, certain I will never look the way these magazines suggest I should. I know that my stomach is bigger than it should be. I know that my thighs rub together when I walk which is far from ideal. I've been told time and time again that only happens to fat people.

I've always been a bit podgy. Even when I was very little there was a fairly healthy amount of puppy fat on you. I was flicking through some old photos recently and I found one of me and my sister when I was about 18 months old and she was probably 7. I already had bigger boobs than her. And those cheeks. Those chobbily cheeks that are cute on a baby, cuter still on a toddler. You can even get away with them as an older kid, you know. Everyone loves a smiling child with cheeks that could move mountains. But they're not so cute on someone on the cusp of adulthood. I think they're going to stay with me for the rest of my life. I reckon I will forever have the face of a child.

It's time I go on a diet. I can't keep going on this way, eating everything and getting fatter by the day. I had a Mars Bar for breakfast this morning for goodness sake. Enough is enough. No-one will ever look at me if my stomach bulges over the tops of my jeans. No-one will ever want to be with me if they see how fat my arms are and how saggy my backside is. As of today, I am no longer eating food. I will eat one apple a day and that's it.

I hate you. I hate everything about you. I hate my square hands and my broad shoulders and my flat feet and my burgeoning breasts. I hate the shape of my hips. I hate the shape of my legs. I hate the curve of my calves and the way my shoulder blades don't jut out at perfect angles. I hate that you can't count my rib bones or the vertebrae in my spine.

I should be able to count my rib bones and the vertebrae in my spine.

I am done with being fat.

Body. I hate everything about you.

***

Dear Body,

Look. Let's face it. I know we haven't always seen eye to eye. We've had our ups and downs, we've had a pretty turbulent relationship. Like most young women my age, I've spent a lot of time considering that you should be a particular way. A particular shape. A particular size. A particular specification to make me the same as everyone else. That was always my main concern when it came to you. Until I was diagnosed with breast cancer a few months ago.

I look back on the way I treated you when we were younger and I feel sad. I'm sad that I treated you with such disdain, that I didn't realise what I had. I regret the hours and days and months and years I spent beating myself up because my body didn't look a certain way. When I think about how I spoke about you, about myself, I realise how terrible I was to myself and there's no wonder I struggled so much with my self-esteem after puberty hit.

I'll admit it. There's a lot I've done to you in the past which would give you reason to be cross with me. The way I treated you when I was younger, starving you of the food and nutrients you needed to grow and to flourish so that I could achieve the "perfect" figure. Now, my love of chocolate probably ticks you off a bit. My penchant for eating a lot of carbs on a regular basis probably makes you crave something a bit greener. My limited exercise for the first 20 years of my life probably, rightfully, left you feeling like I had let you down. My tendency to not look after myself as well as I should when I'm stressed or dejected or exhausted or depressed has probably left you feeling all the same emotions.

Before I was diagnosed with cancer, I thought we were doing ok, you and me. We had come a long way. I'd started doing more with you, thinking a bit more carefully about what I put into you - making sure you got everything you needed to be happy and healthy (but admittedly still eating many cakes and carbs – a leopard can't entirely change its spots). I started to be really bloody grateful to you actually as I felt myself getting stronger. We learned to run. We had spent so long walking together on some incredible journeys. I have always been grateful for my ability to walk. But when we ran, I appreciated you on another level. I began to congratulate my legs for getting me up Sydenham Hill on my 7km run home from work. You let me know about it, but you did it. I started to be proud of the muscles I developed in the pool. I started to look in the mirror and think, "Yeah. You and me. We've got this".

But then you betrayed me. You really bloody let me down when you started growing those poisonous cells in my right breast. They weren't just meek cells either. Though they were but small, they were mighty. At just 22mm they were already Grade 3. Teetering on the edge of being stage 3. Triple negative. Growing quickly. The type of breast cancer most likely to recur. Yeah. Thanks for that. I thought we were friends.

My bitterness towards you comes and goes. I know it's going to take me time to trust you again. But equally I've watched with amazement at how you took on the challenges that came with cancer treatment with aplomb. You were prodded and poked and stabbed and jabbed. You've healed and strengthened and moved on and adapted. Even when you've struggled to heal problematic wounds, you've given it your best shot. Before I even turned 30, I've felt you regenerate and recover from a trauma I never imagined we would know.

You let me down, Body (quite dramatically, let's be frank) but it's you that carried me through treatment. I'm grateful for all the strength we gathered before I got my diagnosis. The runs where I wanted to cry as I pushed and pushed you. The yoga where I amazed myself at the shapes you could twist into. The swims where I ragged you to do a mile in under 30 minutes. It made us more ready to take on treatment and life afterwards together. And while I acknowledge your betrayal, I know that the last few years and those in the future, were and are, as hard for you as for me.

So I guess what I'm saying is thank you. Yes, you betrayed me. But I wouldn't have got very far without you.

***

Dear Body,

Hi. Hello. It's me again. It's a little while since we finished active treatment now. There hasn't been any chemotherapy in our system for a good long while, and we haven't been blasted by radioactive waves recently either, unless you count the ones you're hit with if you stand too close to the microwave. But there have been a hell of a lot of changes that we've had to go through.

You'll probably remember, not long after I wrote to you last time, that I lost my implant. That makes it sound like I just dropped it in the park which obviously didn't happen. It was removed by my surgeon. I'm sure you remember all about that. That was a tough decision for us both, I think. Mentally I couldn't carry on as I was, with little wounds opening up every time I left the hospital, a lengthy stay as an inpatient, neutropenia and a lot of snot and tears in addition. But when I made the decision to have the implant taken out, I never really acknowledged what a massive impact it would have on us. I seriously underestimated what not having a boob would be like. My prosthetic, Gladys, made things look better for the outside world, but for you and me, things were incredibly hard. A chasm opened up between us. Once again, I found us on very different playing fields, but trying out for the same team. I began to disassociate from you. I didn't want to know you. I have been grateful for everything you have done, but after they took my implant, I found it hard to look in the mirror without feeling betrayed and lost and scared and scarred and hopeless. We've had quite the journey, Body. And it's still ongoing.

It sounds like a stupid thing to say, but I'd never really considered my breasts as a particularly big part of my femininity before I came face to face with losing them. Does that sound strange to you? How could I not view them as part of my femininity? They are the definition of what it is to be a woman, right? Wrong, I thought. As the bumbling William Thacker (aka every character Hugh Grant has ever played - is this my second Hugh Grant mention?) points out in Notting Hill, it's not just women who have breasts: "Meatloaf has a very nice pair". So I'd never really linked the two. Maybe it's because I hadn't seen my breasts give life to a baby that I didn't link them with my femininity. But having lost one now, I think I do see them that way.

I'm sorry that you had to go through that. I suppose I could argue that you brought it on yourself by growing those nasty little cancer cells, but that doesn't seem fair really. We'll never truly know why I got breast cancer. It's likely that, given my age, it was just bad luck. And to be honest, I don't think I want to know. Perhaps it was because I ate a scallop on a Wednesday in July in 2011. Perhaps it was because I'm genetically predisposed in a way science doesn't know yet. Perhaps I was working too hard, or perhaps I had inhaled too much of London's claggy, pollution-filled air. Again, I don't know. I think it was just bad luck. I don't think it can really be that you turned on me. Or maybe I do. I don't know.

But here we are. We've been without a right breast for about 18 months, and soon, King K will be trying out a revolutionary process on us to recreate what was lost. It's a technique called lipografting and I'm told that, much like Ron Burgundy, it's kind of a big deal. Every time we have a surgery (and it looks like there's going to be quite a few) there's a gent, known in the clinic simply as The Prof, who will be flown over from Italy to oversee the whole thing. They keep telling me that I'm going to be their model, that I'm going to be "breast cancer famous" and that they'll be talking about us at conferences around the globe for years to come. I don't tell them that while I'm grateful for the surgery and the end of living lopsided that I'd rather not be "breast cancer famous". Alas, it means we're on the way back to being almost "normal" again.

There was a while there though where I didn't think I could face more surgery. There was a time where I found a real sense of understanding you while I was on holiday in Sri Lanka. I'd put curry in you for two or three meals a day. I had hiked through the night, when I never thought I'd be able to withstand anything more than light exercise again. I hadn't taken a prosthetic breast away with me and I felt freer than I had done for a long time. But I was facing a decision. I had a choice to make between staying as I was for potentially the rest of my life, or having an incredibly invasive surgery called a DIEP flap, where I'd need to put on weight, only to be cut from hip to hip and have the tissue extracted from the cut and used to recreate my breast.

By the time I had got back from that trip, I had decided I couldn't face the prospect of intentionally putting on weight. As someone who has constantly battled with food in one way or another, the idea of eating enough to be able to proceed with the surgery filled me with dread. And yeah, while eating everything you want might seem like a luxury that not many can afford, it was also going to be an exercise in reprogramming behaviours I had lived with for the majority of my life. It was overwhelming and terrifying to me, as a person who has gone through various stages of not eating enough and has a tendency to under-eat during times of pressure and stress, to suddenly relinquish control over myself and let go of the food rules I had created for myself. I know that sounds inexplicable. JUST EAT THE CAKE ALICE AND SHUT UP ABOUT IT.

But it was a strange shift for me to get my head around. And by this time, I just wanted to be healthy. I had been to hell and back and I was starting to feel like we were on the same page once again, you and I. I didn't want to put weight on for a surgery that felt so aesthetic. I didn't want to compromise what little health I had regained for a five day stay in hospital and a three month recovery period. So when I turned up to the breast clinic, borderline hysterical about the decision I had to make, almost certain I was condemning myself to a life I wasn't totally comfortable with just to avoid surgery, and King K had a lightbulb moment about a potential other surgery, this newfangled technique called Lipografting that he was pretty sure was going to change the world, I was pretty relieved. And despite the fact I'd settled on us living flat for the foreseeable, I left with an appointment to come back and meet the expert and a date for the first surgery. A new boob, a new recovery and new scars are all on the cards for us.

I think a lot about the scars on you that tell the story of what we've been through, and the scars that are going to come. You see, breast cancer doesn't just leave behind a scar from the life-saving mastectomy. Quite the opposite in fact. You're covered in tiny little pock marks that serve as reminders of everything you've seen and been through. There is obviously the scar which stretches from the right hand side of my breast across into where my cleavage used to be. The way the skin folds over this in the middle makes it look like a crater, formed by two tectonic plates as they have rubbed together. And then there's the spots that mark where tubes were poked into our skin so that extra fluid could be drained into bottles rather than building up in our breast.

There'll be a few more of these to come, despite there already being four as it stands. And a key part of lipografting is the liposuction which will in turn leave little raised bumps on our legs as a permanent reminder of the fat that has been sucked out of you to recreate one of the things cancer took from us. And let's not forget about the indentation in my left arm - the one where a wire was inserted and directed straight through to my heart so that the chemotherapy could be given, removing the need to insert a cannula into already rigid and difficult to find veins. We are covered in little scars and not so little scars that remind us of the tiny details of living through cancer treatment. And that's not even mentioning the emotional scars.

I know that there is still a really long way to go before this reconstruction is finished. They reckon it's going to take about a year, and perhaps five or six surgeries to complete the work. It's slow progress. A softly, softly approach that I'd argue goes against the nature of King K who wants everything done yesterday. And while we're not in for a three-month recovery, like we would be with the DIEP flap, I know from experience that anaesthetic hits hard and I always want to be back on my feet before it's actually reasonable.

So we're in for another long haul experience, my friend. But I feel like we're well practised at that. And maybe, when it's all finished, we'll regain some of the confidence that has been lost over recent years. Maybe I'll enjoy dressing you again. Perhaps I'll re-establish my style and relearn to have some confidence in you and the way you look. Perhaps, perhaps, perhaps.

Now, we wait.

***

Dear Body

I'm back. Here we are. A few months out from what should hopefully be the last of our surgeries for a while. Part of me hopes that this will be the last of my surgeries for forever, but it feels too bold to say that out loud. Since we last spoke, I've had four surgeries to rebuild my breast. There have been more tears than I would care to admit. There has been a lot of snot. There have been cuts and bruises. Bruises like you cannot even imagine. Bruises that contain all of the colours of the rainbow where they've done the liposuction. After the first surgery, they accidentally took too much fat away so had to re-sculpt my bottom a bit. It's peachier than ever.

This technique for rebuilding was chosen because it was deemed to be less intense than a DIEP flap, which, as I mentioned last time we spoke, has a recovery time of three months. While this technique is definitely less intense, it has still been a long and arduous process, which I have been pretty grumpy about at times, especially recently while I've been waiting for the arrival of this next surgery. I constantly fluctuate between hoping it's going to be the last surgery and trying to manage my expectations that it might not be. It's a process which has taken over a year to complete and has left me with many mixed feelings.

You're a bit bigger than I would like at the moment. That feels like an unfair thing to say, but it's the honest truth. I have become squishy around the edges - more squishy than I have ever been before, but when I consider what you've had to put up with over the last year it's impossible to ignore the reasons why this has happened. I've had four surgeries. I have needed to recover. I have turned to food for comfort. I have not been able to move you as much as I would like. And as you well know, I have been completely and entirely knackered. I remember when I used to think I was knackered before cancer. I didn't know what I was talking about. I was delusional if I thought that was tired. Some days now, even all this time after finishing my active treatment, I can find myself struggling to climb the stairs to our flat. I once wrote that comparing tiredness to fatigue is like comparing cricket with moonwalking and I feel like that's possibly one of the most apt descriptions I've ever written. The two are completely incomparable, poles apart. They live on different continents and speak different languages. One is a vegetarian and one is a meat eater. The two could not be more different if they tried. But you know all of this. You know how hard it is for us to make our legs move on the days we're really exhausted. You know that sometimes a walk to the shop can result in a wipeout scenario. You're all too aware that if I make the mistake of, you know, staying up late and having a bit of a life, I'll likely have to spend the next day in bed. It hasn't been easy. And that's without even mentioning the physical things - notably, going back up to two breasts.

I don't know what I was expecting. Perhaps I was hoping for some remarkable transformation in my brain along with my body. That when I was back up to two boobs that I'd be reborn or something. That my confidence would grow and my heart would fill and I'd be able to leave behind some of the stuff I've been clutching onto. But that's been far from the case. It's been no easy adjustment. And I know how ridiculous that sounds. I can hear people rolling their eyes at me for making this into more of a big deal than it needs to be, but it's been hard. Really hard. The surgery hasn't been a magic wand which has been waved and repurposed all of the terrible memories of exploding breasts, cavernous ruins of where the tissue once was, lost nipples and left me feeling satisfied with the replacement that has been carved onto my chest. That's not to say I am not grateful for this pioneering surgery. I am. And I am grateful to go back up to two boobs - but my point is that this surgery hasn't undone everything that has gone before it. Nor can the incredible job my surgical team has done replace what we lost. No matter how anatomically amazing it is, the reconstruction is still a reminder of what happened. It is a reminder that we went to hell and back. A reminder that despite the fact it's coming up to three years since I was diagnosed, it has taken that long to correct the damage that cancer did to my body. And even after that damage has been rectified, it will still never be the breast I lost. Why should I force myself to forget?

Once again, I have been amazed at how you have recovered from the trauma that has been inflicted on you. Over the last year of this reconstruction I have known indescribable pain. The first time I woke up after the lipografting I felt like someone had taken a razor and shaved my legs from the inside, which I suppose they kind of had. After the last surgery, I couldn't go from lying to sitting without crying out. As I sit here now, my breast is heavy with the saline injected into my implant almost a week ago to stretch the skin in preparation for the next stage of reconstruction. It feels alien and uncomfortable. I ache from the discomfort of building up this new appendage and I ache for the days when I didn't have an awareness of the original breast that sat there.

The procedure to rebuild my breast may have nearly come to an end for us, but the procedure to rebuild the other parts of myself that cancer took will continue long after King K tells me he doesn't want to see me for a year.

***

Dear Body,

I have been slipping back into old habits of late, since the I had my final surgery and came home with a new breast. Those habits where I chastise you for being wrong, rather than being grateful for all we've been through and everything you've carried me through. I've noticed myself being particularly hard on the tops of our arms and the size of our stomach. The liposuction we had for the reconstruction means that I gain weight in a different way. It gathers in new places and makes different shapes. Pretty sure I've got a second bum as a result of the way my body has changed post liposuction.

But we've been moving more. And I have experienced some serious moments of absolute joy as I've joined a gym and reminded myself how GREAT it is to move you without being stopped in my tracks by another surgery. I'm learning to work around the fatigue that cancer has left behind. I'm using you to lift weights and hold planks and twist myself into all sorts of shapes I never expected I'd be able to do again. When I hold you in a side plank in yoga with all my weight on the outside of my foot and rooted down through my hand, my hips lifted, I rejoice at your ability to do all these things.

That's not to say I am without pain. Things still hurt a lot. My boob aches pretty much every day. When I lift my arm, you pinch around my armpit - a nervy reminder that things aren't quite what they once were. There's still no feeling where I had a breast and where my fat and implant now reside. We could be prodded in the right tit and never know about it. I regularly get muscular cramping underneath the tiny implant the team inserted and the layer of fat they built up. The team tell me it's my muscles waking up again. I tell them it is so uncomfortable it makes me feel nauseous.

You let me know when I have pushed myself too hard. You force me to stay in bed and rest by giving me a splitting headache and relentless nausea. No more burning the candles at both ends. No more working myself ragged or running round like a blue arsed fly for us. Because the truth is we can't do that any more. We have to be smarter about looking after ourselves.

I know I whinge a lot but I really do strive to have an attitude of gratitude and that gratitude makes its way from my body through every pore in my skin whenever I get sweaty and disgusting in the gym. But the truth is, as much as I wish I'd had a revolution in the way I view you, it changes from day to day. It's a sure fire indicator of the state of my mental health too, to be honest. I'm hard on you when I am engaged in a battle with my brain, because you are the easiest thing to lash out at. Some days I am grateful for you, some days I am worn out by you, some days I am angry at you.

But one thing is for certain, the days I am at home in my body, the days when I feel proud of my size and my shape and my strength regardless of what the world thinks of me, those days are like magic.

Thanks again, bod. For everything you've done in the past and everything we will do in the future. You may not be as strong or as fit as I'd like, but you've had a pretty tough ordeal of late and I suppose, when I'm being reasonable with myself, I can let that slide.

Who knows what the future holds for us, eh?

Please don't try to kill me again.

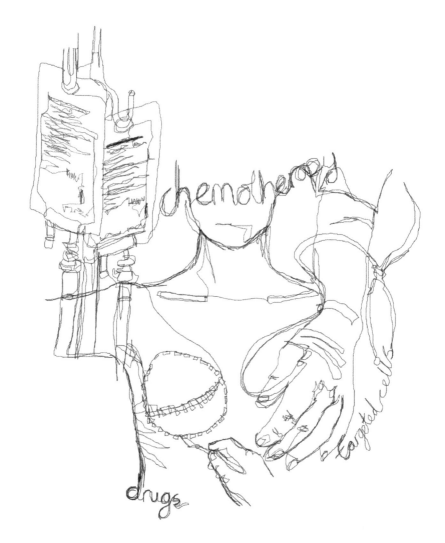

Chapter 12: The Gritty Bits

If you were to ask people - not patients, not those who have been through treatment but just your average Tom, Dick or Harry - which part of cancer treatment scared them, I'd bet you any money they'd say the chemotherapy. Surgery is a big deal. Radiotherapy is often forgotten. But chemo is the dark spectre of cancer treatment that hangs over everyone who hears about it. We've all grown up with the images of people on screens and in books with bald faces and pallid expressions. We've seen clip after clip showing those undergoing chemotherapy hooked up to drips that feed poison into their veins and leave them as a shadow of the person they were before the treatment. We hear statements from anti-medical evangelists telling us it's not cancer that kills people, but chemotherapy. And once you've sat in an oncologist's office hearing the possible side effects that you may encounter after that poison is pumped into your body, but that there's no real way to know which side effects you'll experience, I get that it is pretty scary. But the truth is, that while the impact of chemotherapy is hell on earth, it doesn't always look like it does in the movies.

I mean. Let's not dally about the topic here. Chemotherapy is a massive pile of shit. Steaming shit. But ultimately, it does save lives. But the way it saves lives, and the impact it has on a patient, differs from person to person and from treatment regime to treatment regime. I think it was that uncertainty which threw me most when I was waiting to start my 18 weeks of chemotherapy.

One of the first things my breast care nurse told me on that first day I was diagnosed was that I was going to need chemotherapy. I vividly remember her looking at me and saying, "You will need chemotherapy and you will lose your hair. I want to get that out there straight away". So it was a given for me from day dot. At this point we didn't know whether I would do chemo first or surgery first, but the team knew I was going to need chemo. They'd already told me they were going to play hardball with my tumorous tata. We were basically about to engage in a ferocious routine that wasn't that dissimilar to the games of hockey I used to play at secondary school (side note, I can never understand why secondary schools give angsty teenage girls massive sticks of wood that they can use as a weapon against other equally angsty teenage girls, honestly, hockey was hell at my school). They told me we were going all in on my cancer because I was young, otherwise healthy and I could take it. Going all in meant a bells and whistles approach. A brutal mastectomy. A heavy dose of poison and some serious burning with a radiotherapy beam. Banging.

As a result of that conversation with my brilliant breast care nurse, from the 7th July 2015 I began building myself up mentally, physically and emotionally to start chemo. But as always seems to be the case at some point in everyone's cancer treatment, things didn't quite go to plan. The complications from my mastectomy meant that the start date for my chemotherapy regime was continually pushed further and further back. My stilted recovery from surgery meant that every part of my treatment was shunted. I never thought I'd actually cheer when King K gave me the all clear to start having poison injected into my veins on a three-weekly basis, but cheer I did. Cancer really does screw with your perceptions.

Before my first session, it was weird waiting for something that was going to make the next few months of my life harder than I could ever have anticipated. It was strange to be excited to start something that I was actually completely terrified about. But one thing that I really struggled with was the Great Unknown of what how the treatment would affect me, because there are no hard and fast rules for the side effects that you'll be gifted with once the cytotoxic drugs have dripped their way into your system. The great unknown has never been my friend and chemo was the biggest unknown I'd ever had the displeasure of meeting. If cancer was a squatter in my life, as I described it in the early days, chemo was my unchartered Everest, with no maps, no footpaths and no idea of what was waiting for me at the peak.

Eventually, the date of my first chemotherapy session rolled around. And before they hooked me up, I stood by the window and looked out at the panoramic view of London below me. If there's one thing you don't expect when you're about to undergo chemotherapy for breast cancer, it's to have an incredible view of one of your favourite cities at your feet. But such were the joys of having chemo at Guy's Hospital in 2015.

I'm not sure if you're aware, but I've always been a stubborn old mare. I dread to think what I'll be like when I get older, but adamant I wasn't going to let cancer get the better of me, I vowed on that first day of chemo to take the stairs up to the tenth floor every time I had to visit the chemo unit. I point blank refused to take the lift, whether I was going up for treatment, to have my PICC line (more on this in a mo) cleaned, for counselling or for complementary therapies, I climbed every single one of those steps, flipping the bird to cancer as I went.

My team had planned for me to have six cycles of chemo, with two different sets of drugs. The first three cycles of my treatment were called FEC chemotherapy, because it's made up of three drugs – fluorouacil, epirubicin and cyclophosphamide. The second lot of chemotherapy saw me receive three heavy doses of taxotere (or docetaxol). The FEC made me sick as a dog and my pee red, and the taxotere stole my energy, stamina and, to be honest, for a while there it took a lot of what made me a person.

Chemotherapy, whilst a bit of a swine of a treatment to experience, is incredibly clever. As a person who has always been a bit nerdy about science, I was fascinated to learn about how chemo worked. In laymans terms, the cytotoxic drugs that make up chemotherapy target any fast growing cells in your body. Cancer is a bit of a git in that it usually grows very quickly, so chemo goes after those cells and endeavours to kill them off - but it can't differentiate the bad cells from the good cells that grow at speed - so it blanket targets them all. That's why your hair, skin, belly, nails and many other things are affected by chemo drugs. They can't tell the good guys from the bad guy's, so just go all in and kill everything they can. Clever. But a bit lethal.

Now, there are a few things I believe it is genuinely impossible to talk about if you're going to talk honestly about chemotherapy, and there's a strong chance these might make you feel a bit squeamish. The first, is how bloody (pun intended) hard it is on your veins. The second is the wild and unpredictable things it does to your poo.

Let's tackle the veins first, eh? The thing about chemotherapy is that it is toxic. It is a poison. I have used that word a few times, but lemme tell you once and for all, that is not just hyperbole. Chemotherapy is actual poison which is pumped into your body to target any fast growing cells. It's an incredibly clever little drug (or combination of drugs in most cases) but when it's fed directly into your veins through a cannular, the veins can struggle. Mine really struggled. After just a few sessions my already prone-to-hiding veins became even more difficult to cannulate. It was like they saw a needle coming towards them and decided to retreat like terrified army troops in a bad military movie. It became harder and harder to get a site, not to mention how rigid, hard and painful the veins themselves had become as a result of getting that poison washed through them. I never really thought that veins could hurt, but shortly after my second treatment, I became unable to straighten my left arm for nauseating pain. If I straighten my arm now, even this long after treatment has finished, there's no pain but you can see the trace of my still hardened vein. And I can still remember how it felt.

But this meant that directing the drugs through my veins and via the usual route became out of the question very quickly. Don't make any noises about needing an alternative approach being "typically Alice", it's actually quite a common problem, I swear. It was recommended that I have a PICC line inserted. Now to the uninitiated, a PICC line is a thin, soft, long tube that is inserted into a vein in your arm, leg or neck. The tip of the catheter is positioned in a large vein that carries blood into the heart. The PICC line is used to both put stuff in, such as the chemo drugs and antibiotics which I needed more times than I care to remember, and take bloods out. It made me feel like the bionic woman. The way it works means that the "port" part of the catheter (about 3cm in length) hangs out on the outside of your body, secured against your skin with a plaster. I felt like I had some of my insides on my outsides. But it meant there was no fannying or stabbing around trying to find a viable vein before every treatment or whenever I needed my bloods doing. So being a Bionic Woman, whilst weird and a fairly good party trick, made the whole chemotherapy process much, much easier.

As for the poo, I do not believe anyone who has ever had chemo hasn't had problems with their bottom. Whether it's stuck inside you or coming out at a rate of knots (sorry), chemo drugs really screw with your digestive system. I know this is probably too much information, but the whole objective here is to be honest about this experience and I was pretty distressed by chemo's impact on my belly. Truth be told, the poo wasn't so much of a problem for me, apart from when the constipation started to pass and I managed to make a right old mess of my bumhole by passing what essentially felt like rocks, but FEC in particular took my appetite from me, and let me tell you, that's tantamount to waging war. If there's one time I'll accept the fight or battle analogy, it's when something gets in the way of my voracious appetite. Because that's basically my body's way of flipping me the bird and I do not respond well to that. I became a dedicated follower of the humble garden pea, because there were days when it was the only thing I could face. Pasta, peas and butter became my salvation. I genuinely don't know if I would have survived chemo without peas. And thank goodness, they weren't one of those chemo foods I went off as soon as treatment finished. A life without peas, I would argue, is a very sad life indeed.

Appetite and poo aside, I have honestly never smelled trumps as toxic as chemo trumps. I recently got sent a copy of *F*ck You Cancer* by writer and podcaster Deborah James and when I was flicking through, one of the first things I stumbled upon was her chapter about "chemo farts and other unexpected side effects".

In it she says: "Prepare yourself - and by prepare I mean, get yourself a nose peg, buy a dog and warn everyone who lives with you that due to chemotherapy, your stomach is about to change - and not for the better. You will discover a new-found ability to produce a stench you thought was only possible for a year's worth of decomposing cabbage. The dog is needed so that you have someone else to blame the smell on".

And she's absolutely right. Now this book was written a fair while after I had chemotherapy, so I had no-one to warn me of the way my belly was going to start expelling smells that belong in only the most disgusting of sewers. You remember London's fatberg? That disgusting mass of detritus from the sinks and drains of the city that was found in the bowels of the sewers? Imagine how that might have smelled. Multiply it by about 10 and you're probably somewhere near the gloriously ghastly stench that I was able to produce during chemo. Not to mention the BURPS. They didn't smell as disgusting as the farts, but let me tell you, chemo burps are some of the loudest and most violent burps in the history of the world. And they're uncontrollable. They often jump out at you when you least expect it. On the tube. In the park when you're walking approximately three paces behind a total stranger. In the hospital waiting room. Honestly, when people tell you that there are parts of cancer treatment that are absolutely hilarious, these are the parts they're talking about. There's nothing better than letting out an inordinately loud belch, one that should not come from anything other than an overfed gorilla, and having the person turn around and look at you in disgust for them to recognise immediately that they've just judged a cancer patient and panic-smile sympathetically at you. Small victories and all.

Beyond the poo, the pumps, the burps and the vein issues, the side effects of chemo are many and they are varied. I took a lot of anti-sickness tablets to combat the nausea which was pretty relentless for the first three or four days after treatment, but overall I was fairly lucky. But much like chemo burps, the side effects can crop up with little to notice. I seemed to collect new ones with every cycle. There's the standard nausea, stomach problems and fatigue that everyone seems to get. Then there's the hairloss - not just the hairs on your head but the hairs everywhere else too. My leg hair was the last to go and the first to come back. Why is that?! Then there's some of the more left field treats - like the day I woke up with a massive blister in my nostril, or when the skin around my eyeballs became so dry I started to resemble a scaly pink lizard. The rest of my skin, meanwhile, lost every freckle, every drip of colour and began to resemble tracing paper. Thin, crispy, grey and sallow. Even if I had kept my hair, I think the state of my skin and my steroid induced moon-face would have indicated to the world that I was not a well woman.

And the heartburn! Dear sweet Jesus, I thought I'd had heartburn before. I thought I knew what heartburn was but it was not a patch on this new phenomena I was experiencing. Forget the slightly uncomfortable, warm feeling lingering in your chest and imagine downing several gallons of fire like a confused fire-eater and feeling them rest around your heart, your lungs and in your throat consistently for days at a time. God, the thought of that makes me feel sick as a dog. I can still practically feel the remnants of it. Even years after the fact.

Fatigue was another thing that blindsided me, and continues to do so. Like a car that splutters and groans through the end of the tank of petrol, there's not much you can do when your body gives in to real and honest fatigue. There's something very humbling, and intensely frustrating, at working with a body that can't do what you want it to. There's a lesson to be learned in listening to what your body is telling you and responding accordingly. But it's not an easy process to learn. And often, when you think you're doing OK, relentless fatigue comes along to remind you that you are still being held hostage by a set of parameters that you had no part in defining. During treatment, there were times when I couldn't walk up the stairs, cried out of sheer exhaustion, could barely put one foot in front of the other. There were weeks that passed by in a sleepy haze, where no amount of rest could ease the weariness that pervaded every single cell of your body. I suppose there's no wonder really. When I think about all the hard work my body was doing, healing from the trauma of every fast growing cell being tackled by a chemo-shaped defender, it's no wonder I was tired. Not to mention the healing from surgeries and then any energy I expended trying to exist. My body was really going through the wringer. During chemo, I was the sickest I have ever been, and the sickest I ever expect to be in my life. But that almost doesn't feel like a big enough statement to explain just how poorly chemo made me and continues to make people who are trying their hardest to survive.

I always say that comparing cancer and post-cancer fatigue to tiredness is like comparing cricket and walking on the moon. The two are just so far from being related, it's impossible to put them in the same category. There have been times since I finished treatment when I have done "too much" (which can include spending a day out with friends) and have found myself glued to my bed with a strong chance of vomiting lingering on the periphery. There have been times where my body has simply shut down from being over-exerted. Times when I have barely been able to make it the ten metres from my bed to the bathroom. These things have improved over time, but there are definitely elements of fatigue as a result of cancer treatment that linger longer than you would like. And a big part of making the most of life after cancer is learning that your life now might come with different limits. That has been a phenomenal adjustment for me.

Everyone seems to know that chemotherapy makes you lose your hair. Again, it goes back to the images we've seen of people going through treatment bald and pale and pasty. But the truth is, not everyone loses their hair any more. Scalp cooling (where patients wear a cap which essentially freezes the hair follicles to stop the chemotherapy from targeting them) has been revolutionary for so many people. Blogger and radio presenter Rachael Bland, who I have mentioned many times before, managed to keep her beautiful long locks and her memorial raised over £3000 for scalp cooling. Many other friends of mine have managed to keep most of their hair as they've undergone treatment. But it can have varying results.

Another blogger friend, Em Fisher, who is thriving with secondary breast cancer told me that cold-capping "isn't all shampoo and roses" and added "I know bald is beautiful, but losing 60% of your hair, it being shit, fluffy and nothing like the hair you used to have is beautiful too." And she's totally right. Cold capping doesn't always eradicate the hairloss side effect and regrowth post chemo can be unruly and distressing in its own way. Equally, it can stop you from losing something that can be such a big part of your identity. Ultimately, as with every other part of cancer, there's no wrong or right way to proceed here. Not cold-capping was best for me. Cold-capping was best for others. It's about each individual, and I think that's something we sometimes forget when we're discussing the nuances of treatment.

That uncertainty was what really put me off the idea of ramming what was essentially an icepack on my head for 30 minutes before treatment and an hour after. My hair was pretty thin and wispy and one of the chemo nurses told me that thicker hair tends to have better results. I didn't fancy going through an additionally difficult procedure when no-one could guarantee me it would make a difference. I like hard facts, not "maybe" or "probably". I wanted "definitely". Scalp cooling couldn't give me that.

And so within a few days of my diagnosis, I cut my hair short.

The night after my first chemo my friends came round to give me a buzzcut.

14 days after my first treatment, right on cue, my hair began falling out in clumps.

Three weeks after my first treatment, when the physical pain of my hair follicles dying became unbearable and the emotional pain of seeing the patchy-haired head in the mirror became too much, my Mum shaved my head. Just in time for my second treatment.

Soon enough, I got into a bit of a rhythm. Each treatment came and went. Chris and I developed coping strategies. Do you remember that part in *Harry Potter and The Half Blood Prince* when Harry and Dumbledore go to retrieve the horcrux, a seventh of Voldemort's soul from the cave? And Harry has to make Dumbledore drink all of the potion before they can get the locket? Well, I think drinking on chemo can be a bit like this, especially on FEC. We quickly created what became known as The Dumbledore Deal. Chris became the Harry Potter to my Hogwarts headmaster. His main role was to remind me to keep hydrated even when I felt too sick to drink. "Harry Potter" (and this isn't some weird role play we've continued, I hasten to add) made me drink loads before chemo. He made me drink loads during chemo. He made me drink loads after chemo. And he made me keep drinking, even when I felt, like Dumbledore, that there was no way I could continue drinking.

Then there were the times I would look Chris straight in the eye the night before each chemotherapy treatment, eyes full and bottom lip trembling, and tell him that I didn't want to do chemo again, that I couldn't face it. That I couldn't bear the thought of feeling like hell for a week or longer again. That I just wanted to give up.

He would look me in the face and ask me "Do you want to go to Glastonbury, Alice?" I'd imperceptibly nod. And he'd tell me that, in that case, I'd better buck up, wise up and go to the hospital the next day.

It became our code for "do you want to keep living, Alice?"

Despite it all, despite the trauma and the heartache and the poo issues, the scaly skin and the infections, the spiked temperatures and the hospital stays, mostly, I really did want to keep living.

***

When it comes to cancer treatments, radiotherapy is the lesser-talked-about sibling of chemotherapy. It doesn't have the reputation that chemotherapy does, it isn't perceived to be as blatant in the way it goes about its business and it generally isn't as widely recognised as part of Operation Let's Blast the Pants off Cancer.

But radiotherapy, despite all these things, is still an integral part of cancer treatment for many people and one which can take its toll, if not as much physically as its predecessors then emotionally and mentally. The treatments may only be 15 minutes long, but hot-footing your way to the hospital five days a week for a minimum of three weeks is hardly anyone's idea of a good time.

I was very apprehensive ahead of my first session of radiotherapy. I'd had my CT scan and my planning session. I'd been given three tiny tattoos to mark where the radiation would be focused. The team had all the measurements for ensuring I'd be blasted in the right place and I'd learned the position I'd be spending 225 minutes in over the following three weeks (it's a bit like being in fifth position in ballet, or what your arms would be doing if you were holding a massive beach ball above your head).

I remember taking two photos of myself before I left the house for my very first day of radiotherapy. Bald headed, bewildered and a bit off-kilter looking, I gave a thumbs up in the first, bloody thrilled to have made it to the last leg and flipped cancer the v's in the second, furious to still be going through treatment, fear-filled at what was to come next, anxious about the next set of challenges ahead. I photoshopped a face onto an image of a potato and placed it side by side with the grumpy picture to demonstrate my brilliant likeness to a spud and the resemblance was uncanny.

Before this stage of treatment began I knew the basics of what I was going to be experiencing. But it was quite different when I found myself on that first day, back in a hospital gown, back in a clinical setting, awaiting the last part of my active cancer treatment.

It was quite different when the team, though incredibly friendly and wonderfully reassuring, muttered numbers and words at one another over me in some kind of medical language that I had zero understanding of: 'One right and one ant'.

It was quite different when they shifted me into exactly the right spot on the bed, telling me not to help them, but to let them manipulate my body as they needed to.

It was quite different when they left the room, the risk of them being exposed to what I was being exposed to, too great for them to remain.

It was quite different when the machine clunked and clicked and growled its way around me, blasting The Artist Formerly Known as Boob with radioactive waves, eradicating any final stubborn cancer cells which may have survived the poison of chemotherapy.

Radiotherapy is the last flourish across the finish line, the last push in a pretty brutal series of events. But for many people, the end of radiotherapy and active treatment marks the beginning of something else – a whole new journey, a new set of obstacles, a new bunch of challenges to tackle.

Maybe to onlookers it seems like it's easier than what has come before it. Maybe because it's often the last thing on the treatment menu for most patients, it's expected that the feeling of almost being 'done' will carry you to that victory lap. My victory lap, the last day of my radiotherapy treatment, mainly consisted of a lot of food and a lot of tears. Leaving the hospital with my Mum on one side, Chris on the other and seeing my dad waiting for me at the exit of St Thomas', all of us trying our hardest to keep our shit together.

I found radiotherapy easier than chemotherapy, but it's all relative. No matter what has come before it, finding yourself in that environment will never be easy. It's manageable. But to call it "easy" is to do yourself a disservice.

***

I love quotes. I know everyone says it's basic, but words have always been my bag. I've always dreamed of writing the sort of sentences that hit the nail on the head and pertinently say the things so many of us think. My phone is filled with screenshots of motivational messages designed to the nines saying everything from "hey little fighter, soon things will be brighter" to "let go of the illusion it could have been any different."

I use other people's words as a way to add salve to the little cuts and scrapes of life. From Louisa M Alcott in Little Women to JK Rowling in Harry Potter, or Amy Liptrot in The Outrun, I have always used words as sticky tape over the cracks in my life and my heart.

But there was one quote that stuck with me throughout the gritty bits of my treatment. I think it's the perfect note to end this chapter on. Because cancer treatment is hell. It's really, really shit (the kind that gets stuck and causes you to rip yourself a new bumhole), but it truly is manageable. The aftermath lasts far longer than the actual treatment itself. It is like walking through a shit storm without so much as a raincoat, let alone anything that actually repels faeces, if such a thing were to exist.

But you get through it, because there is no other choice.

"And once the storm is over, you won't remember how you made it through, how you managed to survive. You won't even be sure, whether the storm is really over. But one thing is certain. When you come out of the storm, you won't be the same person who walked in." - Haruki Murakami

Thanks Haruki. You won't know how much strength your words gave me at a time when I really, really needed 'em.

dark days

Chapter 13: The Dark Place

I think I might be a really good actress, you know. I know you're not supposed to say these things. I know it's not the done thing to furnish praise on yourself for the things you're good at. But I think I might be a really good actress. Perhaps I should have chosen that as my career, instead of stumbling into marketing and trying to be a writer. The funny thing is, I did think about becoming a performer. I auditioned for two theatre schools. I had five more auditions lined up. But I didn't feel comfortable with the vibe. That's not why I think I might be a really good actress. I think this because, for the most part, people describe me as the most positive person they've ever met. Or they used to, I suppose. They don't so much anymore, not since I've come out and explained that I take Citalopram every day to try and even out my thoughts. They definitely wouldn't say that if they knew that I had thought, hard and for a prolonged period of time, about killing myself. Looks like I just blew my cover, eh?

Winston Churchill described his depression as a "black dog" though the term is purported to be much older than our war-time Prime Minister. He explained that he didn't like standing too close to the edges of train platforms, nor did he "like to stand by the side of a ship and look down into the water." He explained that "a second's action would end everything. A few drops of desperation." and these words ring very true for me. Journalist and mental health awareness queen Bryony Gordon calls her OCD "Jareth the Goblin King", while my good friend and writer Katie Brennan describes her mind gremlins as her "anxiety goblin". We all have our own names and descriptions for our discombobulated brains. And we all have our own experiences.

I think it's important to be upfront here because I want to be open about my experience of depression. But I'm not going to talk in too much detail about the things I have thought of doing to end my life, because I don't think it's responsible for me to do that, and also, you don't need to know, especially if you are prone to these kind of thoughts too. While I have considered killing myself on numerous occasions, I have never attempted to end my own life, nor have I made plans to do so, nor do I intend to do so in the future. The thoughts I have had have primarily been of the "what if" variety. These have not necessarily just been for fleeting moments either - sometimes many, many moments pass before I can rouse my brain out of the places that take me to a world without me in it. And I'm using the word "moments" here with poetic licence. These feelings can, and have, lasted for hours at a time. Rarely do they last days - the depression may linger but I am lucky in that these thoughts, generally, don't stick around for too long.

The NHS describes the symptoms of clinical depression in a much less creative but probably more effective way as "lasting feelings of unhappiness and hopelessness, to losing interest in the things you used to enjoy and feeling very tearful," adding "There can be physical symptoms too, such as feeling constantly tired, sleeping badly, having no appetite or sex drive, and various aches and pains." Many people before me have written eloquently and effectively about their own experiences of depression, but the truth is every person's experience of depression is different.

For me, the darkness seeps in from the edges before it consumes me, like watercolours on blotting paper. It nearly always hits me hardest as the sun pokes through the bedroom curtains first thing in the morning. When I'm teetering close to the edge of The Dark Place™, it's as though I live my days fighting against it but as soon as I succumb to sleep, it's impossible to avoid it - and that's where I find myself when I wake up.

On those mornings, it's like every millimetre of colour has been extracted from the world. The view from my bed looks like a bad Instagram filter has been applied and then every hint of light has been sapped from it. As soon as I wake into the greyness, I know I'm in for a battle to find the yellows and blues and greens that I so love. I know that no matter how beautiful the sky, or how gorgeous the weather, or how lush the smell of fresh rain is, I will not notice. I will not stop to feel the sun shining on my face. I will not smile. I will barely be able to form sentences as words escape me completely. It will cripple me. Leave me in stasis as I'm unable to put a pair of socks on. I will look in the mirror and not know the person staring back at me, despite seeing her every day for pretty much 30 years. Sometimes, I am so anxious I can't even decide what to buy for tea (dinner if you're not from the North) because I am overwhelmed by the fear of what might happen if I pick the wrong thing. The world has never ended as a result of a bad culinary decision. In my right mind, I know nothing terrible will happen, but in those moments, I do not know for sure.

Writer M Molly Backes describes this stasis as "the Impossible Task". In a thread of tweets from August 2018, she explained: "The Impossible Task could be anything: going to the bank, refilling a prescription, making your bed, checking your email, paying a bill. From the outside, its sudden impossibility makes ZERO sense.

The Impossible Task is rarely actually difficult. It's something you've done a thousand times. For this reason, it's hard for outsiders to have sympathy. "Why don't you just do it & get it over with?" "It would take you like 20 minutes & then it would be done." OH, WE KNOW.

If you're grappling with an Impossible Task, you already have these conversations happening in your brain. Plus, there's probably an even more helpful voice in your brain reminding you of what a screw up you are for not being able to do this seemingly very simple thing."

Depression, when it is at its very worst, clutches at my rib cage, constricts my heart and makes me gasp for air. My breath never reaches beyond my shoulders, clamouring somewhere around the top of my chest rather than filling all of my body. My body itself feels alien to me, as though it is moving independently from my brain. The two couldn't be further away from each other, despite being fundamentally connected. I always say it's like wading through treacle on the dark days. My limbs know that my brain is telling them to put one foot in front of the other but it's unable to respond to those messages in real time. It's like there has been a breakdown in the system that connects the two and the messages aren't getting through properly. Like my body can hear them, but can't process them properly. The wires short circuit somewhere around my hips and I am almost completely immobilised. It feels like I will never know the ease of movement again, like I will never feel any feeling other than hollowed-out emptiness again. On the worst days I wish I could feel sadness. It would be a relief from the relentless nothingness of the monotone day. And the worst part? I don't know how far in I am until I have come out of the other side. I don't remember that there are better days ahead, nor that there have been better days in my past. I can't remember that there is life beyond the black cloud that is engulfing me. I don't see how deep I am in to the forest or how much I am missing the daylight until I find my way out of the dangerous tangle of branches and step, blinking into the warmth of the sun. The darkness is all encompassing. It is suffocating. It takes away rationality and reason, replacing them with inaction and lethargy. This all sounds like hyperbole, but it isn't. It sounds like I'm plucking at these descriptions from a bag of carefully curated metaphors. But this is how it feels to me.

Alongside my depression, anxiety plays a heavy part in my mental health issues too. I never realised how anxious I was until I spoke to my first CBT practitioner. But before I arrive at The Dark Place or as I move away from it, my mind goes into overdrive. This intense activity leaves barely any space for the thoughts that are there already, let alone those that are necessary to function as a human being. My mind feels like an old antique shop, filled to the brim with nick-nackery that is useless and taking up too much space. My anxious thoughts are like wind-up toys with a broken mechanism - there's no point to them. They are just taking up space. Valuable space. A goblin sits in my cranium eating away at my sense of reason. He tells me no-one cares what I think. He tells me I am untalented and unremarkable. He is hard to ignore.

But, as with most things, these feelings (or the lack of feelings) do not last forever. Sometimes they stay for 24 hours, sometimes they stay for a couple of days. At times they linger for weeks at a time. Eventually, they pass, often slowly, leaving me shellshocked and exhausted. And if I'm lucky, the distance between me and those feelings is a big one. The Black Dog finds his way to a faraway field and leaves me in peace, preoccupied by a bone or another dog or a rabbit. But it's only with the beauty of hindsight that I can now see the times I thought it had buggered off to a different field, when in fact it had only moved into the next room, or gone for a brief nap. Is this metaphor going too far? I can't tell.

Hindsight is a wonderful thing and I see now that in the past, even when I thought I was well and doing ok with my mental health, I wasn't. Depression might not have been right there at the forefront stealing my emotions and robbing me of my joy, but while I was in treatment, it was never that far away. For the first time in a long time, there's some real distance between it and me at the moment. Dare I say, perhaps the Dog is even in quarantine as its made its way to a different continent? I don't know how long it will last, but I am revelling in it while I can.

I'm wary of falling back on overused metaphors when talking about depression and trying to explain it in terms that are easy to understand if you're lucky enough to never have experienced it. It's so much easier to talk about cancer - because that's a term that everyone gets. Cancer = a tumour. But depression is so multifaceted it's hard to pin down. And perhaps someone reading this who has experience of depression will not recognise any of the symptoms I describe. No two people are the same and with an average human brain made up of about 100 billion cells, I'd argue that no two brains are the same either. We are complex creatures made up of complex needs and desires and emotions and these differ so much from person to person - so why wouldn't our mental health experiences be different?

Depression, for me, is like an ocean. Not in every way, because I consider the ocean to be one of the most beautiful and relaxing things on this mad old planet we happen to live on, but it's an easy metaphor to turn to because while beautiful, the water is volatile and changeable. Depression is, more specifically, like the waves of the ocean. The currents vary. The tide shifts. It's never the same and it's difficult to predict the changeability of it, without a tonne of scientific interventions. Some days, the good days, I can sit in the shore and watch the waves from a distance. I know they're there. I can see them on the horizon, but they're not getting all up in my grill. Sometimes, the water winds its way around my feet and laps at my ankles. These are usually the days when the darkness begins to creep in. When the peripheries of my life begin to smudge with darkness. Then there are the days the waves are bigger, have more impact, making it difficult to stand. Then there are the days when the waves are taller than I am. Their force is overwhelming. They push and pull in every direction and I am powerless beneath them. These enormous waves knock me down and pull me under.

It's a weird analogy, I guess, if you know how much I love the sea. And if you don't, lemme tell you, I LOVE the sea. I am never happier when I am on, in or near water but I was always raised to recognise the dangers that hide below the surface and respect the waters. The undercurrents that can rip you from safety to danger in seconds, or the waves that can lead your legs to buckle. And while depression doesn't share ANY of the positive points that massive bodies of water do (it is not beautiful, it is not serene, it does not offer a place to feel alive, quite the opposite in fact), the similarities between The Blues of the Brain and the darker blues of the ocean are many.

I have always managed to drag myself to the surface after being submerged. I reach the air, clamouring for breath but remarkably unscathed, all things considered. But one of the things that constantly drives me to keep pushing out, to fight the brutal currents that could easily drag me down to nothingness is the people I love in my life. There have been times when I haven't wanted to continue, where I have wanted to cease existing. There have been times when I could easily have given in to the surge of the waves and allow myself to be carried away by depressive thoughts and suicidal ideation, but my anchor, the thing that keeps me hanging on, are the incredible people I have found myself surrounded by.

This ocean analogy was borne out of a way to explore depression, to give it a comparison which those who hadn't experienced it could identify with but I think beyond that there are many parallels which can be drawn between this and making my way through the hardest days when I was in treatment. Because there were times then when I thought I wouldn't, couldn't make it through the gruelling reality of breast cancer treatment. You've heard the expression "breast cancer isn't pink and fluffy"? Well those very bleak days when my breast exploded again and I couldn't see the point in carrying on prove it. The time I had to practically crawl to the toilet in the middle of chemotherapy, or when I could barely climb the stairs and couldn't see a time when I'd ever feel well again show that breast cancer is so much more than a ribbon. I look back on those times and realise how lucky I was that those waves of depression which came frequently and relentlessly did not consume me or take me down a path to a really terrible place.

This feels very exposing to write and the actual writing of these words is laced with the guilt I've spoken of so much before. How selfish am I to think about dying, to think about taking my own life when there are people out there striving to survive? Doing everything they can to fight for another day on Planet Earth? But

I'd never say that to anyone else with mental health issues. I don't know if you've noticed but I don't hold myself in the same regard as I do other people. I would never dream of saying a person who took their own life was selfish. I'd say they were desperate and desolate and heartsore and broken. But I do not afford myself that same thoughtfulness.

No matter how far I am into the quagmire of my own brain though, I can still usually see that there's something worth getting out of it for. My therapist asked me once what stops me from following through when the really dark thoughts come to mind and they are manyfold. I have a husband who loves me and who I adore. He laughs at my jokes and fills the cracks in my broken heart with gold dust. I have a family who are completely mad in their own way but fiercely loving and supportive. I have friends who have gone above and beyond for me. I have so many sunsets yet to witness. So many sunrises to catch. There are so many places in the world I have left to swim. There are places I need to explore, new friends I have yet to meet, cats I've yet to stroke. Songs I have yet to hear which I will need to sing at the top of my voice and so, so many books I have to read and allow their new worlds to unfurl around me. I need to keep living for the long summer days of June that stretch on endlessly and the cold, fresh, crunchy winter mornings where the light glistens on everything it touches. I keep going because there are delicious things I have yet to taste, so many memories left to make. I have so much left to give.

Even in the darkest of times, there are still many, many reasons to keep living. If you've been desperate and desolate and heartsore and broken, or if you're any of those things now, take a breath. Take a really deep breath, close your eyes and look for the reasons to keep going. Because they are there. They are waiting for you. And they'll be all the sweeter when you can feel them in the hairs that stand up on the back of your neck and see them with a heart that's as open as your eyes. There is so much left to live for. There is so much left to get out of this world. And we deserve every minute of future joy that is waiting just around the corner.

Chapter 14: Finishing Treatment

When I was a kid and we first got the Internet at home, I was transfixed by looking at the BBC's On This Day website. This was, of course, in the years before MySpace came into existence and I found myself wasting time choosing apt song lyrics to express the depths of my emotion and deciding which of my friends should be in my top nine, not to mention being distracted by the politics of being a teenage girl. But before all that, when things were a bit simpler, I think On This Day was probably the website I visited most. I used to sit and read about all of the things that happened on specific days in history. What happened on my birthday. What happened on mum's birthday, on dad's, on my sister's. What happened on Christmas Day in 1973 or at the turn of the century. We had this enormous book called The Chronicle of the 20th Century which I used to pore over for hours at a time, devouring news articles and headlines from specific days of specific years in history. And it wasn't even because I was a history buff who was obsessed with history lessons at school. While I found that part of the book and the internet interesting, I was more fixated on the idea of anniversaries than anything else.

We all have anniversaries or days that we mark, whether they're personal like birthdays or wedding anniversaries or the anniversary of losing a loved one; or whether they're more generic days celebrated by everyone – St Patrick's Day, New Year's, Armistice. But when something happens – like in my case, you guessed it, you get diagnosed with cancer - you're given a whole new bunch of anniversaries to celebrate. Scratch that. I'm pretty sure celebrate is not an appropriate word for all of them, but there are certainly days that stick in your mind, like heavy concrete boulders in the road, after you've heard those words.

The anniversary of the day you're diagnosed. The day you had your first (hopefully only) surgery. The day you started chemo.

The day you shaved your head. The day you finished chemo. The day you finished treatment. And almost inevitably, because I am prone to excessive rumination, all of these days stick in my head. I never know if they're happy days, sad days or a combination of the two. Sometimes I'm not even really thinking about it but I wake up and feel a bit strange and it takes me a couple of hours or a couple of days to notice the date and realise why (I can still blame that on chemo brain, right?). And every time one of these anniversaries comes around, I feel simultaneously like 30 seconds and 30 years have passed since whichever anniversary it is.

For a long time, I thought that 25th March 2016, Good Friday, marked the end of my treatment. It was the day of my final radiotherapy. It was the day my family and I went out for a lovely dinner to celebrate the end of a gruelling time. It was the day that my "active treatment" had ended. I can remember every single detail of the morning leading up to my last radiotherapy session. I can remember what I was wearing (red polar neck top, jeans, silk headscarf, red lipstick and big earrings if you were wondering), I remember sending Chris to find the nurses I'd seen every day for three weeks to give them a box of biscuits – a small token of my gratitude for making one of the weirdest times in my life seem more normal. I remember lying on the table, arms above me, thinking about how far I had come in the ten months since they said I had cancer. I wore red lipstick – the best armour I know – and I tried my hardest not to cry as they blasted me with a final dose of radioactive waves, the last my right breast will ever receive. Until recently I thought that this was the end of my treatment, but in fact, the end of treatment came many, many months later, over two years after finishing my final radiotherapy.

There are not many things I know about myself, other than that I make great bread, a cracking cheese sauce and I have the ability to turn a phrase. But even as a person with the words and an all right way of moulding them into written sentences, explaining the way I felt on 2nd August, 2018, when my surgeon finally told me he didn't need to see me for a whole 12 months is impossible. I shared a photograph on Instagram that I took in the moments after I left the breast clinic, face full of tears with a contradictory smile. I wrote the caption: "The overwhelmed and happy tears of a person who just got told they don't have to be back at the breast clinic until August 2019. After three years of being in and out of there every two to three months this marks the end of my treatment. While my "active" treatment ended in 2016 with my final radiotherapy session, the last 18 months have been a slog to make it back to some semblance of the body I began with. It is a monumental day. It was a monumental moment when I shook my surgeon by the hand and said "see you in 12 months". There are times I never thought I would make it. But I am here. I am here."

I've actually been putting off writing this chapter for a while, but I only realised why when I got kicked out of the breast clinic and told to disappear for 365 days (pretty much exactly). Because yes, I had finished my active treatment. Yes, I had begun the process of moving forwards from that part of my treatment, but there was still so much left to do after 25th March 2016. I had a whole boob to rebuild. And I knew that that process was going to be long. The reconstruction process I undertook to get back to a person who had two boobs rather than one boob and a vacancy where the rest of my chest should have been extended my treatment beyond that.

Breast surgeon and co-author of *The Complete Guide to Breast Cancer*, Liz O'Riordan, who is also a member of the Breast Cancer Club (a club no-one ever wants to be part of) described her treatment as a triathlon, made up not of a swim, a bike ride and a run, but a surgery, a chemotherapy programme and several sessions of radiotherapy. This analogy is so dead on. For many, there's another part of treatment in the form of ongoing hormone therapy, or others like me who have to undergo further surgery, or like Liz whose cancer comes back in a local recurrence and have to engage in another round of activity. There are others who never get to say that they are finishing treatment. But if you have a diagnosis of primary breast cancer and your treatment is straight forward, it is very much a triathlon of being cut, poisoned and burned but perhaps with a long walk tagged on the end.

All things considered my triathlon went pretty smoothly, exploding breast, multiple surgeries and two episodes of neutropenia aside. Actually, when you put it in those terms it doesn't sound like it went that smoothly. But it did. The actual tumour was removed with "good margins" meaning there were no little bits left lingering behind. There were "micro-metastases" in my lymph nodes, meaning the cancer had begun to spread from my breast (which is what made my staging 2b-3), but these should have been blasted by the chemotherapy and any lingering cancer-y cells should have been mopped up by the radiotherapy. I was only physically sick three times during chemotherapy and only admitted to hospital for a long stay once. My hair came out in clumps, but my legs have never been smoother than when I was on chemotherapy. There really is no smooth like Chemo smooth, I'll tell you. My skin and nails suffered as the drugs attacked any fast growing cells in my body, unable to differentiate between the good and the bad. Radiotherapy left my skin burnt and sore but aloe vera saved me. My heart, my brain and my body took a battering time and time again during my active treatment. But I survived. And I came out the other side.

But what does finishing treatment really mean? How can it be explained to someone who has never been through it? I read something that compared the end of cancer treatment to the end of a war – the "battle" has been won, the soldiers have gone home, but the battle site is still covered in debris. Things need rebuilding – but rather than putting streets and houses and communities back together, people who've had cancer are putting themselves back together, one piece at a time. We are rebuilding confidence – in ourselves, in our bodies, in our abilities to work or do exercise or to love. We are rebuilding trust in our bodies that they won't betray us again. In some cases, we are still literally watching our bodies being rebuilt. We are watching scars heal and we are trying to move forward while the shadows of the battle linger on. I have written pretty extensively on my thoughts and negative feelings to the often pulled out war analogy that comes with a cancer diagnosis, but in this instance, it's actually completely fitting. My body has long felt like a war-zone in the aftermath of cancer treatment.

Not long after I finished my active treatment, I looked up "survive" in a dictionary, seeking solace in my life-long companion of words. The verb was defined as:
Survive:

- To remain alive or in existence.
- To carry on despite hardships or trauma; persevere: families that were surviving in tents after the flood.
- To remain functional or usable: I dropped the toaster, but it survived.

I remember feeling afraid of adding the term "survivor" to my lexicon, and I still don't trust that there's not something terrifying and tumour shaped around the corner but I am gradually moving further away from "cancer patient" status and into the realms of "cancer survivor". I've never been a survivor before. And to be honest, I don't feel much like a survivor. The word feels weird on my tongue, my fingers don't type it smoothly, even now. Three years after diagnosis and two years after completing my active treatment.

Of the three definitions above, I have felt most like the toaster since finishing treatment – like I'm just about staying functional, moving from day to day in a bit of a haze, burning things a bit in the aftermath of the incident. It's a balance between allowing myself to feel all of the emotions I need to feel, making it through every day, getting out of bed each morning and being grateful that this part of my story has ended this way, rather than any other. While I'm trying to process all of the emotions around what happened over the last few years, I'm plagued by a feeling of guilt. I shouldn't be crying over the end of my treatment, for being sent away from the breast clinic, because for some people their treatment never ends.

I've explained how my mental health has always been volatile and in the aftermath of cancer this hasn't changed. It has neither got worse, nor improved. I'm perpetually hard on myself for everything in my life. I spend a lot of my days consumed with anxiety and warding off dark thoughts that often pervade my sunny exterior – but often only when I close the front door and find myself at home, in my safe place. And talking about all of these cancer type things, and living in the middle of all of these things is so important for the mental healing I'm working on, but it's also sometimes completely overwhelming. Sometimes the tears come and there's nothing I can do to stop them. I cry because I eat too many chocolate fingers. I cry about cancer, I cry about the scars my body is covered in, I cry out of fear for the future, I cry for all the other people in the world I know and love or have spoken to who are going through cancer treatment or have been through cancer treatment. I cry for all of the women in the world who have developed secondary breast cancer and know that ultimately the disease I have survived for now, will kill them. I cry out of sheer exhaustion. I get embarrassed that I'm still so tired, even though I'm "supposed" to feel better now (though it's never clear who says I'm supposed to feel better). I feel like a failure when I see other people who've been through treatment or are going through treatment smashing life, doing all of the great things, without being shackled by a need to hop into bed at approx 9pm every night. I think "I should exercise more, I should eat better. I should try not having as much sugar. All of these things would help me."

The reality is though, there is no right or wrong way to do cancer, cancer treatment or recovery. You've got to do what works for you. Maybe that's screaming and crying and punching things. Maybe it's putting it in a box and pretending it never happened, or maybe it's talking about it and educating people about it. Some people throw themselves into helping others by volunteering, while others concentrate on getting their own lives back on track. There's always such an expectation that cancer survivors should live their lives in a specific way once they're finished treatment, but expecting everyone to run marathons or volunteer or raise oodles of cash is unreasonable. No two people are the same, and no two experiences of cancer are the same - so how can we expect everyone to respond accordingly? It's unrealistic. I will say it again - there is no right or wrong way to do cancer, cancer treatment or recovery. And just because my way is different to your way, it doesn't mean either one of us is doing what we shouldn't do. After cancer it's more important than ever to choose the narrative that works for you - how you tell your story and how you move on from your story is down to you.

I know there are many people who think that having finished treatment, I've left too much of myself in the cancer world, but I'd argue that being told I had cancer was only the introduction to the story. Treatment and what I have done and continue to do beyond that is the crux of my story - the "conflict" if you will, if we're thinking about it in terms of a novel.

Since being sick, something I've really struggled with is whether I'm "letting" cancer "define" me. The inverted commas around both of these words is important – because I think they both carry a moral judgement. Both have agency attached to them. Both have negative connotations. Because in "letting" cancer "define" me, I'm passing the power from my hands into the "hands" of a few mutated cells (ha – that's quite a funny image. A tumour with hands) and allowing them to control the narrative of my life. It is something we are told we must not do. "We must not let cancer define us because then it wins". There are countless articles on the internet telling us just that or celebrating those who haven't been reduced to their experience of cancer. And I celebrate that if they feel good about it. But I don't believe that is true for everyone, nor do I believe being "defined" by cancer is necessarily a bad thing. My career is so intertwined with my life outside of working hours now. And a big part of that is my experience with cancer. It's led to me writing this book, it's all over my social media channels, it's smattered across the internet on various websites. It's allowed me to share my words in some of my favourite publications. It's afforded me some wonderful opportunities.

To say I am "letting" cancer "define" me comes with a myriad of problems because it suggests that there's nothing more to me than cancer. It doesn't allow for my beliefs or my personality traits to come through. There's no space left for the other experiences I've had. And that word "letting" suggests a weakness in a way.

As part of the bigger picture though, would it be a bad thing to let cancer "define me"? It's a thing that happened. It's a big thing that happened. And it has dominated my life for the last three years. It changed my life. So, by definition, doesn't that mean it has defined me in a way? Why does it have this negative connotation attached? I mean, other than the fact that it's a thing that tried to kill me. Obviously that's not so great.

Cancer comes up for me again and again. It is pretty much unavoidable. I know this isn't the case for every person who has experienced cancer, but it is the case for me. It is so intrinsically linked with pretty much everything I do that I really care about. It's why I'm a Boobette for CoppaFeel! It's why I am a trustee for the charity. It's why I am self employed. It's why I can't commit to working more than three days a week right now. It's why, for almost three years, I was in the hospital every couple of months. It has changed my view on the world, it has changed my view of myself. It has changed my relationships and altered my heart in ways I never could have expected.

I don't know if cancer has defined me. I am a person who has had cancer. And it has had a huge impact on my life. But I am also a wife, a sister, a daughter, a friend, a writer, a copywriter, a social media manager, a journalist, a blogger, a lover of the sky. I am passionate and I am humble and I am grateful and I am a maker of great bread. I am a person who loves to read, who loves to write, who loves to cook, who loves thirty second dance parties and singing at the top of my voice. I am a person who has survived cancer. I am a person who lives with cancer in their life, even though the cancerous cells have gone. But I cannot be reduced to just one thing. Humans, by their nature, are multifaceted. So even if cancer comes up in conversations with new people and even if it's the thing they remember after meeting me for the first time, the more they get to know me, the more they'll unravel the layers.

No matter what narrative I choose for my cancer experience, no matter how much it impacts my life beyond my treatment, maybe I am defined by cancer, maybe I am not. Either way I am so much more than my experience of cancer. I am so much more.

Finishing treatment is so often seen as the be all and end all of a cancer "journey". It's the thing you're told to aim for when you are diagnosed, but for many, it's just the beginning of a new process. The start of a new evolution I guess. The day I finished radiotherapy, the last part of my triathlon, I felt like I had won the lottery and had the rug pulled out from beneath my feet at the same time. After three weeks of daily hospital visits and after ten months of treatment, I was exhausted and wanted nothing more than to leave that part of my life behind. I was jubilant at the idea of not needing to be poisoned or burned any more - but I was also terrified of the uncertainties that were to come. I'd come to rely on the regularities of treatment and found comfort in the medical teams I had seen regularly. They were the soldiers who had been fighting for me and now it was left to me to run the clean-up operation solo. I had to make my way back onto the rug that had been so unceremoniously ripped from underneath me, but my first mission was to find it and repair the moth holes and wear and tear it had undergone since we'd parted ways.

Don't get me wrong - finishing treatment is a big deal and it is a great thing. It is a bloody colossal achievement that should be marked and you should feel proud of. My last radiotherapy and then being discharged from the breast clinic for 12 months are signposts in my life that mark the end of the most difficult things I have ever endured - but those signposts also point towards uneasy futures which have involved a tonne of work to unravel what's gone on and apply the plasters and sutures to the emotional and mental scars that cancer leaves behind.

Being diagnosed is one thing, going through treatment is another but probably the biggest part of my experience has been this bit - the aftermath, the moving forward, the moving on. The making my way back to a life which has been irreconcilably changed.

And let me tell you, that's a whole other challenge in itself.

Things I Wish People Knew About Surviving Breast Cancer

**This is an exact copy of a blog that I wrote in August 2017. It is by far one of the most-read posts I have ever written. Looking back at it now, I can see how angry I was. It was like a throwback to teenage angst and Regina George shouting "NO ONE UNDERSTANDS ME" in Mean Girls. But the truth is there are so many people who understand and writing this post proved that to me. I wanted to include it here because this is one post I have written where I have had tonnes of responses from people saying "omg, me too" and I wanted anyone who has had these feelings to know there's a whole army of us stood right behind you.

More and more people every year are being diagnosed with cancer, in one form or another. Whether it's lifestyle, environment, diet or any other factors that is causing the increase is very much up for debate, and not a debate I have enough authority to cast my opinion on. But with every new cancer diagnosis, research and treatments are vastly improving too. Now, if you're diagnosed with primary breast cancer, you have an 80% chance of surviving 10 years after your diagnosis. Fewer people (though still too many) are dying of cancer but we still don't know what to do with survivors. The NHS is often too stretched to support people with the mental, physical and emotional turmoil that cancer leaves behind and not equipped to provide the kind of spiritual support people need after going through a life changing experience. So more and more people are surviving cancer, but their needs are often not understood – even by those closest to them.

In the 17 months since I finished treatment, there's so much I have learned about "surviving" cancer and I thought it might be good to share these with you – so if you're undergoing treatment, or know someone who is, you might get a better idea of what it's like when you're released back into the world. If you've been through treatment, some of these might seem pretty negative – but I think it's important to normalise what life's like after cancer so that if you feel any of these things (and you might think they're all WRONG), you won't feel alone and scared and worried and all the other emotions you experience in The Aftermath of this Life Changing Big Deal thing that happened to you. Buckle up campers, this is a long read.

1. When I say "I'm tired" I don't just mean I didn't get enough sleep last night. It's not because of the antidepressants I take. It's not because I need to eat more veg, or get more exercise (but I should probs get a bit more, shouldn't we all?). It's because these days, post treatment, I reach a point where I splutter to a grinding stop like a car that's been running on fumes for the last 20 miles. I crunch to a standstill with zero ability to continue, no matter how hard I try. Nausea. Headaches. Dizziness. Feeling faint. The works. There's tiredness – which I was very familiar with before cancer – and then there's fatigue and comparing tiredness to fatigue is like comparing cricket to walking on the moon.

I know lots of people who've had cancer treatment don't find that their fatigue lasts as long as mine has and I am a) jealous and b) want to know all their secrets, but for many people who've been through cancer treatment fatigue lingers for various reasons. The day my friend Izzy came round and did all the dishes I'd let build up because I was knackered was one of the best gifts she could have provided. She told me she found it therapeutic but I know she was doing it because she knew what a difference it would make to me. These things make a difference, no matter how long it is since you've finished treatment.

2. Survivors guilt is real. Real and pervasive. Every time I hear

about another person, whether I've met them, kind of half know them or have never heard of them at all, who has been diagnosed with secondary breast cancer or have died from it, I get a little crack in my heart. These cracks deepen the more of this news I hear. I wonder why I was, for now at least, more lucky than them. I wonder why I deserved to survive. I feel an overwhelming sense of responsibility to them to be better, to do more, to make the most of the life that I've been given. I feel guilty for still talking about my experience because at least the active part of treatment is over for me. What about the thousands of other people for whom treatment will never end? They don't want to hear me wanging on about this when I'm lucky enough to have wrapped up my treatment.

There are people literally fighting for their lives and sometimes I feel like I should sit down and shut up because my opinion of cancer isn't relevant because it's not trying to kill me. I remember when my article was in Red I got shouted down by a handful of people who thought my experience wasn't valid and that they should have been telling the stories of people with secondaries instead of me. So often I don't understand why I am still here and so many of my amazing Boobette sisters are not. It's a bloody minefield – especially if you're prone to excessive rumination like I am. Survivors guilt is real and will bring up a range of unruly emotions in you. Accept them and remember that you're doing the best you can.

3. Cancer never really leaves you. Long after you've finished treatment, cancer has a way of rearing its ugly head and infiltrating on the life you're trying to rebuild. Whether that's annual checkups at the hospital that give you palpitations, nightmares about it coming back, scares about recurrences and the feelings of fear, sadness, heartbreak and everything else you

feel are constant reminders of what happened to you. Sometimes I have flashbacks to things, traumatic moments of when I was in treatment, that I've blacked out. Sometimes these thoughts hit me like a punch to the temple and other times they just wash over me. I can never judge which way I'm going to react or how I'm going to feel when this happens. But they tell me this is normal.

Don't forget about what happened to us. We don't need sympathetic head tilts but don't panic if we tell you we're still thinking about cancer 5 years after diagnosis. Ask how we are – and not in a perfunctory greeting way. Really ask. If we're ok, we'll tell you. But if we need to talk, that question will feel like a life ring being thrown out to us in the middle of a black and stormy ocean, where we've been floundering miles from the shore.

4. I have strong opinions about the language around cancer. I HATE THE FIGHT ANALOGY. I hate the idea that if you die from cancer you "lose". How can you lose when you're giving everything you have? How can you say people have "lost their battle" when they were never armed with the right infantries to battle with. Cancer is like Danerys on Drogon, leaving devastation in its path but cancer is never the victor. And it doesn't matter how hard you fight. Even the best will in the world, the strongest positive mental attitude doesn't stop cancer cells from multiplying – it's medicine that does that. And we are not in control of how our bodies react to medicine (whether traditional or alternative, whatever your choice). People die. Don't use euphemisms. It does them a disservice.

5. I think about death. I think about my death. I make jokes about dying. And that's ok. I don't need you to tell me not to talk like that or to "stop thinking that way". Talking this way is one of my self defence mechanisms and it's one I really, really need. It might

seem negative or pessimistic but it's the way I'm dealing with this. I know it might be hard for you to think about my cancer coming back. I know it might make you uncomfortable when I crack jokes about not making it to 40 years old, but if I'm laughing, you can laugh too. Laughter is the thing that has saved my life. The reality is that cancer might not just make the one stop in my life and I'm coming to terms with that. I know it's hard for you too but it's how I'm going to survive the uncertainty.

6. It doesn't end after radiotherapy finishes. Having had triple negative breast cancer means I don't have any further lines of defence against breast cancer but for so many, taking daily Tamoxifen, a hormone suppressant for five or ten years after finishing active treatment is a reality, meaning their treatment continues long after that last blast of radiotherapy. Other breast cancer's need to be treated with a drug called Herceptin which is usually injected in the months following active treatment. Then there's the fear, checkups, post-traumatic-stress, depression, anxiety that comes with life after treatment. There's so much more to cancer than just the treatment part of things.

7. I don't give a hoot where you keep your damn handbag. And putting a heart on your wall to create breast cancer "awareness" is a sure fire way to make me give you a lecture on how to actually check your tits. Memes about how much you hate cancer are useless and to be honest, kind of offensive sometimes, unless they're saying that you hate cancer and we all need to do our own bit to make sure we're doing what we can to make sure we get treatment asap if we do get cancer. That was a long sentence but what I mean is, I'm only interested in memes that tell us what we should be looking out for when it comes to signs and symptoms of cancer, rather than just an "I hate cancer" meme. Dude, I'm pretty sure no-one likes it much.

8. Finding yourself might not be as easy as you hope, but you'll get there a little at a time. And you'll surprise yourself frequently by your ability to pick yourself up and get on with shit even when you feel you cannot any more. I still have no idea who I am after cancer, so much so that when I am asked for an interesting fact about myself, it's all I have to do to stop myself from blurting out "I HAD CANCER" because I feel like it's a huge part of who I am/ was/will be in the future, but also, that's not ideal when meeting new people. They'd think I was bonkers. They can wait to find that out.

It is over three years since cancer first appeared on the horizon of my life, before it proceeded with its mission to rip its way through my life like a hurricane. Did I mention I'd had breast cancer? Probably just the once or twice I guess. I do try and keep it under my hat. But here we are. Three years. Everything and nothing has changed, all at the same time.

I think there was a part of me that hoped that when I had finished treatment, the depression would go the way of the cancer. That it would be eradicated, not by drugs, but by the fact I had been through something so massive, it would quiet all of the irrational thoughts that wriggle their way into my consciousness on a regular basis. There was a part of me that hoped that when I had finished treatment, I would become some kind of strength paragon - that I'd never find my way back into the cellar of my mental state where the cobwebs thicken and linger and the blackness is all encompassing.

Before I got sick, I was of the perception that everyone who had experienced a cancer diagnosis discovered a newfound joy de vivre after seeing their mortality dangled before them as the result of a tumour hanging out somewhere in their body. I thought that everyone who went through cancer treatment was some kind of superhero who found life after cancer nothing but "easy, breezy and beautiful" (to quote makeup brand Covergirl's strapline - I've watched a lot of America's Next Top Model in my time, ten points if you got the reference without being prompted). But I have found that could not be further from the truth. I don't speak for every cancer patient and I'm sure that there are many who will disagree with me, but if I expected my depression to be cured by my cancer, I couldn't have been more wrong.

The truth is, the enormity of going through a cancer experience, especially when you're younger I think, never really leaves you. It leaves holes in your heart, chips in your personality, scabs on your brain, and chinks in the armour of your emotional resilience. It leaves its marks on your skin, a brown smudge on your career and shards of its existence in every aspect of your life. There's so much talk about "the new normal" that comes after you've survived cancer treatment - the idea that patients have to come to terms with the fact they'll never be the same again - but in fact, I believe that after cancer, there's no normal any more. "Normal" has been ripped into a thousand pieces and discarded like yesterday's newspaper. "Normal" is old news that cannot be re-experienced. As with most big events in life, you cannot go back to the way things were before, it's about learning how to deal with the new set of parameters you have been given. From learning to deal with new health anxieties, to experiencing post-traumatic stress disorder, being struck by survivor's guilt, figuring out what the hell you went into the kitchen for when chemo brain strikes, learning your fatigue levels and re-establishing your position within the working world, it's an absolute minefield.

And all of these things, rather than decreasing my mental health issues, have contributed to exacerbating them. I have found life after cancer to be so, so much harder than life when I was in the middle of treatment. I hoped I'd discover that oft peddled newfound zest for life we're trained to expect from cancer "survivors". And while I could argue that I have in many ways (jeez, don't even get me started on how much I love the sky, you'll instantly regret it), it'd be remiss for me to not acknowledge that mental health struggles continue beyond cancer treatment. Immediately after I wrapped up my final radiotherapy, I felt that I should be revelling in the dawn that came with completing treatment, but in reality, the darkness came. And it has taken a long time for it to recede. This isn't an uncommon reaction to finishing treatment for cancer either. In a report compiled by cancer support charity Macmillan in 2013 (*Cured But at What Cost*), they explained: "Cancer and its treatment often leaves a gruelling physical and mental legacy for many years afterwards", adding that the "true cost of cancer" was yet to be fully understood. The research goes on to explain that around 240,000 of the 2 million people in the UK who are living with or beyond cancer are also living with mental health problems, which can include moderate to severe anxiety or depression, and post-traumatic stress disorder (PTSD). So in answer to the question, "shouldn't you be less depressed now?" I'd be inclined to argue there are many more reasons for my depression than there were before - but that gets us into a whole causality debate which gets tricky when it comes to mental health issues. For many, and for me before treatment, there was no "reason" for me to be depressed, but I still had depression.

Cancer fear and anxiety are a match made in hell too by the way. I had never had any kind of anxiety about my physical health before I got sick, which is ironic really when I worried about LITERALLY EVERYTHING ELSE and then it was my health which actually became problematic.

I had Triple Negative Breast Cancer (TNBC), which means it's not responsive to hormones. According to Cancer Research, "Triple negative breast cancer is an uncommon type of breast cancer" and is one "whose cells don't have receptors for the hormones oestrogen and progesterone or the Her2 protein". For every type of cancer, there's a different treatment regimen, and unlike other kinds of breast cancer, there's no second line of defence after finishing primary treatment. Patients with other kinds of breast cancer are given drugs to help keep the cancer at bay by blocking hormones or controlling cell growth and repair. There is nothing like this for TNBC. It is usually more aggressive than other forms of breast cancer (who knew there were many types of breast cancer?!) and is apparently more likely to come back than others for the first five years after treatment finishes. It's also more likely that any recurrences will be metastatic - meaning that the cancer has spread beyond the breast and become incurable. That's nice for someone who suffers with anxiety, isn't it? Especially when cancer makes you anxious anyway. I'm currently learning to live with an anxiety that is essentially on steroids. Regardless of what kind of primary cancer you had, or have, I know from speaking to others that I'm not alone in how incredibly difficult it is to shake the fear of recurrence. Every time there's a niggling pain or a cough that lingers a bit longer than it should, a post-cancer mind often veers headfirst into thoughts of metastatic recurrence. A few months ago, I developed an ongoing pain in my collar bone. A daily discomfort that played on my mind so much that even a clean bone scan hasn't totally appeased the feeling that a few wayward cancer cells have hunkered down in my clavicle. I criticise myself often (isn't that new and unique for me?) for becoming a hypochondriac who panics about every little change that happens in my body but I'm trying to reframe that. I am not a hypochondriac. I am hyper-vigilant. And getting it checked is the smart and sensible thing to do. RIGHT? I don't know. But I'm told that the fear eases over time.

None of this is to say life after cancer is more miserable than life before cancer. Far from it. It's just different for me. Change isn't all bad (apart from the dramatic and unprecedented alteration of the Cadbury's Creme Egg recipe in 2015 or the resizing of Toblerone in 2016, both of which were unacceptable. Stop messing with chocolate, manufacturers). My life has changed irrevocably since 7th July 2015 and many of these changes have been positive. If it wasn't for cancer, I wouldn't be sat here on this blissfully sunny day in July in 2018 letting the summer breeze wash over me through the window and contemplating my cancer experience beyond what happened to me. I'd probably still be working in a job that didn't fill my heart or drive my soul, not writing a non-fiction book funded by 176 heroes who believed in this project. I'd probably still have to sandwich myself in between sweaty armpits on my commute into work. I'd probably have watched a lot less Gilmore Girls. I'd probably have said the word "boobs" significantly fewer times. But in reality, many of these changes I've experienced cannot have a value placed on them - they are neither positive nor negative. They just are. They are the tremors that are felt as a result of the butterfly wings flapping a lifetime ago.

I never want anyone to think that I am ungrateful for the opportunities I have been given - from being put on notice that life doesn't last forever, to being happy and healthy and sitting here writing this book. My survivor's guilt is real and pervasive. I am constantly reminded how lucky I am to be alive and well. Even when I'm reflecting on my situation in what might not seem like the most positive light, I never do it without telling myself how far I have come. I know it might seem like I'm complaining about life after cancer when I share things on social media but I cannot articulate effectively how much I value the fact that I am alive and cancer-free. I am constantly reminding myself that I am lucky - but this is a tool I often use against myself too. "BUCK UP, PRIVATE," I tell myself. "YOU'RE ALIVE, AND AS FAR AS YOU KNOW THERE'S NO CANCER IN YOUR BODY SO WHAT THE HELL DO YOU HAVE TO WHINGE ABOUT?" It's true too, but it's not the be all and end all of my experience. "The Guilt" is something else I am learning about all the time, but it's something I feel keenly, something I do not need to be reminded about. I feel guilty that I'm whinging when I shouldn't be, that I have only had primary breast cancer when so many others have it so much worse, that I have survived when so many others do not. But I really am doing the very best I can. I'm working on being the best survivor I can be, and I'm working on getting my brain onto an even keel too. But it is ongoing work. And I think the "after cancer" bit is often forgotten by those who haven't been right there in the trenches.

A CBT practitioner approached me at an event a few weeks ago and offered me the most elegant and eloquent metaphor for life after cancer I've ever heard. It's the sort of metaphor I wish I'd come up with, but I didn't. She explained that from her point of view, going though cancer treatment is a bit like being thrown off a cliff. You fall a huge distance, your body is thrown against the cliff-edge as you tumble, you hit branch after branch. You are battered and you are bruised and you are broken. But you've got to the bottom and you're alive. And the alive bit is what everyone outside of your experience focuses on. Because for the most part, they can't see the damage that has been done. It is hidden under clothes or under "positive thinking" or a feigned smile. And of course being alive is WONDERFUL. It is a GIFT. But being alive doesn't make what happened any less traumatic. It's easy to forget the fall, the journey, while looking at the survival

On 2nd August 2018, I finally made it to the very bottom of the cliff. I'd been hanging on somewhere in the middle, clutching onto branch after branch that had taken on the form of my lipografting reconstruction. I don't think I was ever particularly honest about how hard I found the reconstruction process, until King K told me I didn't need any more surgeries and I cried for about 24 hours straight. It is a long time since I have cried that much. I cried so much I made myself dehydrated. I am quite surprised I didn't wrinkle up like I'd been in the bath for too long to be honest. But the process to get my body back to some semblance of the body I began with was a long one. It took 14 months and five difficult surgeries. After three years of being in and out of there every two to three months the day King K told me I didn't have to go back to the breast clinic for a year marked the end of my treatment.

I always talk about the exceptional care I received from King K and the team at my hospital, but it's also important to stress here how excellent the mental health care I have received from both my hospital and my primary care team has been. I know that not everyone in the UK has access to the incredible support I have been granted. That's a whole other issue for another time perhaps, but over the last four years, I've had countless appointments with my GP to discuss my mental health and manage my medication; 18 sessions of cognitive behavioural therapy; 7 sessions of mindful cognitive behavioural therapy (M-CBT - basically CBT but using meditation as a tool for managing anxiety and depression) and about 14 counselling sessions with a specialist cancer-care expert. I have had access to practitioners who have helped me begin my mental cancer healing process and open my heart to whatever comes next. I have gone from 10 to 20, 20, 30 and 30 to 40mg of citalopram, guided by the GP's to find a level that works for me. A few months ago when I saw another doctor, I told him I didn't think I was "over" my cancer experience and he replied by saying, simply, kindly, "of course you aren't". All of this care has helped to save my life.

The question "so are you better now?" comes in various different forms. "Are you in remission?" "Are you cancer free?" "But you've got the all clear now, right?" And the answer is less straightforward than I think many "survivors" know how to deal with. How do you explain the nuances of cancer treatment and the fact it's a wily beast who could rear its ugly head again at any time it feels like it to someone who just wants to hear a "YEP. Cancer free and LOVING LIFE"? How do you explain that while the surgery you're having is purely for "aesthetic reasons", it's about so much more than the way you look? How do you explain that you feel like you've been on fire for the last three years, that you don't know who you were before cancer so how the hell can you know who you are after cancer? That your career has been on hold and you need to work out how to make a living that isn't punctuated with surgeries and six weeks of recovery time every few months. These questions about recovery, as with most things post cancer, come from the very best of places. The people asking it want you to be better. To be healed. And the honest answer is too long to explain without being on the receiving end of a lot more questions (at best) and a glazed over expression or swift topic change (at worst). So we, as the patients, reach for comforting words, words that appease their worries, rather than feeding our own needs.

This happens with mental health chats too. People want to know if you're ok, but very few people really want to know the intricacies of what's going on in that bulbous appendage at the top of your body aka in your head. Neither of these observations are criticisms, I know all too well that if I answered "how are you?" honestly sometimes, it'd make the question poser run for the hills. I don't judge them for it, because sometimes what's going on up in there makes me want to run very, very far away from myself too. Timbuktu, anyone?

The value of someone asking these questions and listening attentively to the answers can make a massive difference. I have one friend who has become impervious to my "yeah I'm fine OMG HAVE YOU SEEN THIS FUNNY DOG" brush offs. She'll let me talk about the funny dog (she'd be a fool not to) but then she'll ask me again if I'm really OK. That second question is like a little nod which says "I'm here if you want to talk. I've got you. I'm ready if you need me." It's such a tiny gesture which has consequences which reverberate into every part of my life. But equally, she doesn't push it if I clearly don't want to talk about what's going on.

Every person finds their own variation of what works for them when they're asked this question, whether it's relating to cancer, mental health or another part of their lives. One thing I do know though, is that opening up and talking about these things with a trusted person in your life can make a massive difference. The mental health resources in this country are stretched (understatement) and while talking to a friend or loved one doesn't replace the need for medical intervention in some cases, it can be a good starter for ten in others.

I've said this once, I'll say it again. I do not speak for every cancer survivor. I do not speak for every person who has had depression or lives with anxiety. I'm not here to tell you how to think or how to feel about your own experiences. I'm here to tell you how I feel about my experience of those things in the hope that my truth helps you see yours more clearly, or can offer a bit of solace to you at times when things are tough.

I guess what I'm trying to say is that going through trauma changes a lot. Yes, maybe it has changed the way I look at the world, but the truth is, even three years on from my cancer diagnosis, I'm still trying to unravel the strands of trauma that have knotted their way through my body like a venous system of lessons to be learned. And to the question, shouldn't I be less depressed now? Maybe I should but to paraphrase former president Barack Obama and his exceptional victory speech, depression doesn't care "who you are or where you come from or what you look like or where you love. It doesn't matter whether you're black or white or Hispanic or Asian or Native American or young or old or rich or poor, abled, disabled, gay or straight". It doesn't care what you've lived through or what you've seen. If you have had clinical depression in the truest sense of the word, it doesn't just go away. It takes time and energy and dedication and attention and work to deal with. And cancer just throws a whole heap of stuff on top to unpick.

There's a lot I don't know about life after cancer. There's a lot I am still learning. I get new lessons on how to live in this post-cancer, living-with-depression world, every single day. The "moving on" part that people talk about is still relatively untouched terrain for me. Unchartered territory and I do not have a map. Balancing "lucky" with "grateful", "traumatised", "sad" and "a bit cheesed off about the whole thing" is an act I still have to perfect. It will be a long time before I am able to join the "moving forward" circus with these elements in equilibrium. But I'm trying.

When someone asks "So - are you all clear now?" I will tell them I am in recovery. I am recovering. When someone asks me how I am, I will tell them I am trying. I am doing my best. On the days when I really, truly am no more or no less than "fine", I will revel in the normalcy of it.

There were a lot of times when I didn't think I would make it here. But I am here. I am here. That is a victory.

You're here too. I'm sure there have been times you thought you wouldn't make it either. But here we both are in this weird, wild and wonderful world. Hanging in there every day.

That is a victory, my friend.

How To Survive After Surviving

I'm not alone when I say that "surviving after surviving" has been incredibly difficult for me. And I know that everyone has different experiences so I wanted to take this opportunity to share some of the wonderful wisdom from others who have been in the same boat. I mean, you've got a whole book of my thoughts so I should shut up and let other people speak.

Some of these are my wonderful Boobette pals who work with breast cancer awareness charity CoppaFeel! to spread the good boob checking word and some are people who have used the organisation Trekstock which looks after the "Lost Tribe" or those diagnosed with cancer in their 20s or 30s. Obviously, I know a lot of breast cancer folk so there's a fair few from that club in there, but there are people who have had other experiences of primary cancer too. I'm so grateful to everyone who shared their thoughts here.

- "See a counsellor specialising in people who've had/have serious illness. Don't dismiss the idea - park it, even if you don't do right away." **(Julia, founder of @BCCWW on Twitter)**

- "Find your happy place. Remember what used to make you happy as a child...running, arts, painting, reading, and put time into this. Continue treating yourself with kindness - take yourself out for coffee and cake!" **(Rhyan)**

- "Try yoga or any other form of meditation. Understand that feeling so confused about life after cancer is completely normal. And understanding that being a 'different you' is also completely normal and not always a bad thing." **(Shelley)**

- "I threw myself back into anything that felt 'normal'. For me it was going back to work and being around colleagues. When I was first diagnosed I was off for a month and was climbing the walls at home. Being in work gave me the freedom to escape the world of cancer and talk to people about something totally unrelated. I really missed the routine of this." **(Sam)**

• "Accept that things have changed. Don't beat yourself up if you can't multitask or keep going as you did before." **(Tracie)**

• "For me, a big thing has been having the strength to admit when I am finding life difficult. I've learnt not to brush the overwhelming days off but to embrace them and accept that not every day after cancer is going to be a good or an easy day." **(Diana)**

• "Bringing the horizon in. Something that really helped through treatment was taking each day (or hour/minute when needed!) at a time. Such a cliche but really worked for me. I find focusing on now helps manage the uncertainty about the future. It also helps slow down time and makes me remember and appreciate each day/moment. It's definitely been my main lesson from cancer and am trying to make the most of the 86,400 seconds in a day without planning too far ahead! Either way, whether I get sick again or stay well, worrying about it is just a pure waste of those seconds." **(Sarah)**

• "Be kind to yourself! And the worst part is actually after you finish treatment and the bubble and support has gone. The meditation app Headspace has been amazing for me." **(Donna)**

- "The hardest thing for me has been having to admit when you're having an "off" day, when you're finding it all a bit overwhelming and just having to take a step back and regroup every so often! I find yoga and meditation help to calm my mind, while exercise really helps to keep my mental health on track." **(Sara)**

- "Recognise where you are in terms of energy levels, and make conscious choices about what and who you want to prioritise. I spent a lot of time and caused myself a lot of heartache trying to do everything I did before I got sick at the same ludicrous pace, and in the end found a therapist to help me come to terms with my new normal. It's still a work in progress, but things feel a lot better now I'm taking time to rest rather than throwing myself gungho into working overtime and committing to unrealistic social plans!" **(Catherine)**

- "Writing down how and what you're feeling has been key for me. I wrote a blog throughout my treatment, which I shared on social media but this isn't for everyone. I actually kept many of the posts I wrote to myself and I still do now. I found it a great way to process how I'm feeling and it's also a great way of rationalising your thoughts when you can feel them spiralling out of control-kind of like a self monitoring system to keep you in check." **(Sarah)**

- "For me I think a big part of looking after myself was learning to be a bit more selfish and doing more things for me. I have learnt post diagnosis that it is okay to say 'no' sometimes and to really focus on what feels right for me rather than trying to please others. I still find this difficult and ten years on is a work in progress." **(Jessica)**

• "I've found that I was kinder to myself immediately after treatment, and the more time that has passed, the more I've put pressure on myself to return to "normal". Every now and again, I need a reminder that I'm still making micro-adjustments to accept my new "normal", and though that can be frustrating, it's entirely ok." **(Han)**

• "Tune back into your gut and intuition it will tell you some great things about the potential decisions you want to make (but might be a little scary too). Don't be forced into making changes you don't want to make or think you should because you've survived - do what you need when you need, you can still be a little selfish. Don't compare yourself to other survivors. Acknowledge that this could be a new stage of survivorship. Celebrate that it's over but know that you're still able to ask for help and think about it all - now is when the processing is likely to take place. You will be stronger than you ever knew. Unfortunately this is usually only tested when you have a crappy day, but please remember it. And get enough sleep." **(Emily Hodge, life coach and cancer survivor)**

• "Don't expect too much of yourself emotionally. One of my colleagues said ' you'll never go back to the person you were the day before, and that's ok' and I think for me personally this really rings true. I have tired, emotional days where I feel isolated and scared and just upset and I'm learning to roll with these. I wish someone could give me a rule book for what to do after cancer but they can't so I'm trying to make my own." **(Rachel)**

Whether you've had cancer or not, I think there's a lot that can be taken from this list of glorious ways to take better care of yourself.

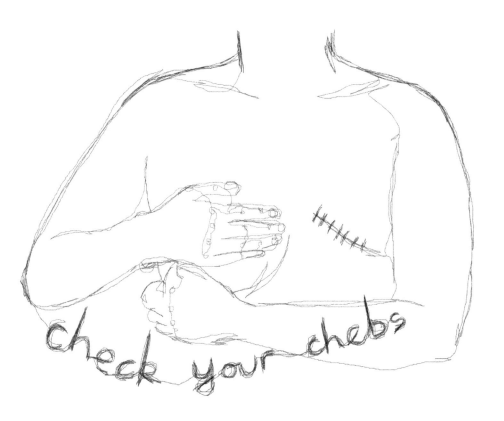

EPILOGUE

Here's the thing, friends. For me, this is the most important part of the book. If you ignore every other part of me baring my soul in the previous 15 chapters (and thanks for sticking with me to the end), I hope that you'll pay attention to this part.

I'm currently sat in a Costa Coffee (other coffee shops are available) having spent the morning representing my pals from CoppaFeel! at the launch of their latest corporate partnership. I'm still £500 off the target for a Kickstarter campaign I launched five days ago - you know, the one that will hopefully have made this book a reality. But I'm sitting down to write this chapter first. Because I really believe in what I'm about to tell you. That sounds like I don't believe in what I've written before now. I do, obviously. But this bit is especially important, so pay attention.

There are a few things that I think it's important that you know about my experience of breast cancer and depression.

Firstly, I was in the habit of checking myself. I don't know why, but I was. Maybe it was seeing the incredible Kris Hallenga (founder of CoppaFeel! But if you follow me on the old socials and don't know that yet, where have you been?) in her documentary *Dying to Live*. Perhaps it was because I'd read Alright Tit, author and writer Lisa Lynch's blog when she was alive. I've never been able to exactly pinpoint why I was doing it. But the fact that I was checking my breasts on a regular basis meant that I knew what they usually looked and felt like. Knowing what my breasts usually looked and felt like meant I recognised when something wasn't quite as it should be. When I felt that hard, pea-sized lump in my right side boob, I knew I hadn't felt it there before. I didn't know how long it had been there. I didn't know what it was doing there. But I knew it wasn't part of the usual make-up of my boob.

I genuinely believe that finding this lump when I did saved my life.

But there was another thing that saved my life too. I was all for leaving this lump and not getting it checked out. I was so cavalier about getting it checked out, you'd think I'd just found a new freckle on the end of my nose after a long, hot summer, not discovered a hard and noticeable lump in my breast tissue. I knew all the signs and symptoms of what I should be looking for when checking my chebs, but I still thought that I could ignore one of them when it tiptoed into my life. It was only because I mentioned this lump to my Mum and Chris that I got my finger out and went to the doctors. I didn't even entertain the idea that it would be cancer, so I was adamant I didn't need to get it checked out. But the truth is, if I hadn't got it checked out when I did, we could be looking at a very different scenario to the world I'm living in now.

Three weeks after I was diagnosed, when I had my lump removed, it was 22mm, pretty tiny in the grand scheme of things, but it was already grade 3, stage 2b/3, meaning the cells were very differentiated from the normal breast cells and it was making its way beyond the breast. There are only three grades of tumours. Grade 3 means it was feisty. Like me. But more deadly (unless you've seen me when I'm hungry). There were also micro-metastases (little cancer lurkers) in my lymph nodes, meaning the cancer had begun to make its way around my body. Because I was diagnosed quickly and began treatment quickly, these micro-metastases have, hopefully, been stopped in their tracks. If they'd been left to their own devices, there's a strong chance those little cancer lurkers would have made a home for themselves somewhere else in my body. Perhaps they'd have settled down in my bones. Or maybe my lungs. Or anywhere really. When cancer settles in these places, it becomes secondary breast cancer, stage 4 breast cancer, incurable breast cancer. Basically, it becomes something you live with for as long as possible. But, like a less glamorous version of Cinderella, there's often a time limit on how long you'll be staying at the party.

Getting diagnosed when I did means that hopefully those micro-metastases have been blasted into oblivion by chemo and won't show their faces around this town again. It meant my cancer was treatable. Curable.

I genuinely believe that going to the doctors when my Mum told me to saved my life.

Both of these things together should mean that cancer will hopefully just be a chapter of my life. Not a very pretty one. Not a very exciting one. Not one that I'd care to re-read. The pages may be dogeared and worn as I go over that part of my life and try to move forward. But it's simply a chapter. One part of the story. Hopefully that story will have many more chapters. Hopefully it will be a well-lived, well-read story that lasts for a long time. Not an epic, but a story worth telling. And for that, I feel incredibly lucky.

Depression, I think, is a different kind of book beast, if we're sticking with that analogy (and why wouldn't we, when I like books more than I like most things, even my husband** some days). It's not a chapter. More an over-arching theme in my life. I find it very interesting that it took getting and dealing with breast cancer for me to be open about my ongoing battles with my brain. There was a point, shortly after I had the idea for this book that I laid in bed and thought to myself "there's no way I could write about how depression and cancer mix". The prospect of talking so openly about the demons that hang around in the dark crevices of my mind terrified me, significantly more than opening a dialogue about my breasts did. While I was going through treatment for breast cancer, I wrote about my fanny openly. I talked about poo. I talked about exploding breasts. I openly and candidly discussed my fertility. But talking about depression? No. I couldn't do that. Definitely not.

But it's true that talking about depression genuinely saves lives, much like knowing your own body can save your life. One in four people will have mental health issues in their lifetimes. Not many fewer than the one in two people who will develop cancer in their lifetime. In 2015/16, 1.4 million people in the UK were referred for talking therapies. It's a much more widespread problem than history would have us believe. So why do we all struggle to stand up and say "Hey. I'm actually really struggling right now"? Why are there people literally dying as a result of their silence?

It took a lot for me to open up and write a blog post called "Confession Time" where I told everyone who read it that I had fought with depression and anxiety for most of my adult life. But do you know how many people came to me and said "Oh. You too? Yeah. I've got depression as well" and immediately we were less alone. I know there are people who think you shouldn't talk about your mental health and the state it's in, but I am not one of them.

Talking isn't an option for everyone though. Sometimes reliving the places your brain has taken you in the past (or even where it is taking you in the present) can be painful. Like standing on an emotional plug that's been left upturned on the bedroom floor. And for some people that pain is too much to take. But I think knowing that the option is there to talk is half the battle. The more we can open up the conversation around mental health, the more those people who don't want to talk can still know that they have someone to talk to when they want to, even when they feel like they don't.

I think cancer and depression threatened my life in the same way. Cancer was a more obvious threat to my life. But depression has threatened my existence on more than one occasion. True, the tumour that grew in my breast tried harder to kill me than I've ever tried to kill myself (a reminder - I have thought about it, but I have never prepared to kill myself) but neither has a monopoly over the threat they made to me staying alive.

It's said a lot, but we Brits are fundamentally disengaged with our peers when discussing emotions. We're an army of people who believe wholeheartedly in the idea of a Stiff Upper Lip. When I was growing up, my parents often said that they were "fine", then jokingly added that was actually an acronym for "fucked off, insecure, nervous and exhausted". But, perhaps, we can start a little revolution for those who are finding things difficult. The next time someone asks you how you are, answer honestly. Don't just revert back to "yeah, good thanks, you?" if you're actually struggling with something internally. I'm not suggesting you give a full breakdown of your emotional state and stability to the guy you buy your Cadbury's Dairy Milk from on a Thursday evening on your way home from work (though, pretty sure we've all been there, amirite? Or is that just me?), but be honest with your friends. Be honest with your family. Be honest with your partner. Opening up and saying "actually, I feel like I am drowning" is the first step to being thrown a lifebelt. No-one knows you're drowning if you don't wave at them on the seashore.

So, what am I trying to say here?

My message is simple. Check your boobs. Know your body. Recognise if anything is unusual.

Don't listen to your brain when it tells you you're a failure. Know that you are not alone. One day you will be able to recognise and differentiate between the depression that is holding you hostage and the rational mind which is the one you should pay attention to.

The gremlins in your mind are bullies. Their main intention is to destroy you. But they're not you. They are as much part of your illness as my tumour was part of my cancer. They do not define you. You are going to be ok. Anyone who has ever been where you are is right behind you. And we believe in you.

You're doing great. However you feel, whether you're living through cancer or mental health issues, you're doing just fine.

Please keep going.

I'm right here with you.

A few thanks…

This book has not been easy to write. Nor was it easy to make happen. I am so grateful to **every.single.person** who pledged or shared the Kickstarter which funded the first print run. Every pledge, regardless of its size let me know that there was someone out there telling me that they believed in what I was doing, and as a person who has a tendency to beat myself into a bloody, bruised and battered mess (metaphorically) this was a constant driver to me to keep going when I didn't believe in myself. You are all incredible humans. Thank you for every message of encouragement, every timid "how's the book going?" and every nudge when I needed one. Thanks for taking a punt on some words that I put on a page.

Obviously, I have to thank the love of my life. The person who holds me up when I feel like I cannot stand and the person who knows me at my very worst and my very best. You have made me the best person I can be and without you I don't know where I'd be or how I'd survive. Thank you, Teddy Edward. JOKES. I mean you, Chris. You're the actual light of my life. You're my lifebelt. You're my hero. And you make a really good Sunday roast.

Thanks also to Georgia, without whom this book wouldn't be the beautiful thing it is. And without whom I would never have believed I could make it myself after I learned I didn't have enough social media followers for a mainstream publisher to take a punt on me. Thank you for being my cheerleader and thank you for sharing your obscene artistic skills with me on this project. You really are the best friend a gal could ask for.

As this hasn't been a traditional publishing process, I've had to improvise a bit with some of the tricker parts of the process -

namely proofing and editing. Sometimes when you've written something, you become totally blind to any spelling or grammar issues and you no longer notice if sentences don't make any sense. So thank you to Jenny Baker and Karen Troman for their help on this, and to Sophie Oldridge for being my BETA reader.

And I must mention Sophie Trew, the kindred spirit who has constantly been my cheerleader - a tour de force who makes the world a better place and has helped me power through some of my darkest and most twisty cancer-related thoughts. I keep a postcard from her that tells me to "ignore the negative committee that meets inside my brain". I think that's a bit of advice we could all do with taking.

Thanks to all the incredible people in my life I have met as a result of my cancer treatment and my depression. I know that the longer I live as a person who has had breast cancer, the more people I'll meet going through the same or similar experiences, and the more people I'll encounter who don't make it through. The more often I'll hear of the deaths of those for whom treatment didn't work as well as mine seems to have done. But one of the redeeming features of being diagnosed with cancer is the people you meet. Incredible people who have lived through the same sort of experiences as you. And while the risks of losing these people are almost tangible, not surrounding yourself with these people for fear of loss would be foolish. Because they are your tribe. Because you can learn from them. And if it weren't for cancer you never would have met them. So to my fellow Boobettes, Alex, Laura, Sarah, Vashti, who aren't here any more, to Janine and Emma, my fellow Breast Cancer Care models who died while I was writing this, to the inimitable Rachael Bland, to Dean Eastmond who faced his diagnosis of Ewings Sarcoma with strength and dignity and humour until the end, to Sharon and to

Margot, and to anyone else who has died as a result of this bitter and scathing disease. Thank you for being a part of my life. You are all missed.

Thanks also to my paternal grandmother, Constance Alice Mary Purkiss, without whom I don't think I ever would have discovered my love of words and writing. She bought me my first thesaurus and moulded me into the spelling and grammar pedant I am today. She died while I was writing this book and I loved her very, very much.

I can't mention everyone I'd like to thank. I haven't even finished the book yet (no lie, did the epilogue first innit) but I am #blessed with some insanely wonderful people in my life who help me through the darkest of times and laugh with me through the very best of times. I hope you know who you are when I say thanks to you here.

[Insert prayer emoji]

Onwards, with hope.

Resources

For cancer

This is a list of websites and blogs that helped me when I was going through treatment and beyond.

www.alicemaypurkiss.co.uk/category/cancer/
www.jennybaker.org.uk
http://coppafeel.org/ (GREAT for how to check your boobs!)
www.breastcancercare.org.uk
www.breastcancerhaven.org.uk
www.maggiescentres.org
www.dimblebycancercare.org
www.livebetterwith.com
www.coachingemily.com (Emily is a wonderful coach and guide who has her own experience of cancer)
www.abcdiagnosis.co.uk
www.sophiesabbage.com
You, Me, Big C Podcast
www.girlvscancer.co.uk

For depression

www.samaritans.org
www.mind.org.uk
www.blurtitout.org
www.nhs.uk/conditions/cognitive-behavioural-therapy-cbt/
www.time-to-change.org.uk
www.together-uk.org/
www.rethink.org

If you are in distress, please either call your GP and request a same day appointment, or call The Samaritans or Mind.

If you feel you are a risk to your personal safety, **go straight to your nearest A&E**.

Books for Both

Late Fragments - Kate Gross
Mad Girl - Bryony Gordon
Sane New World - Ruby Wax
Reasons for Staying Alive - Matt Haig
Furiously Happy - Jenny Lawson
The Year of Magical Thinking - Joan Didion
A Beginners Guide to Losing Your Mind - Emily Reynolds
Awareness - Anthony Mello
How to Heal Your Life - Louise Hay
Happy - Fearne Cotton
When Breath Becomes Air - Paul Kalanithi
The C Word - Lisa Lynch
Do What You Want - Ruby Tandoh

Books that are about neither breast cancer nor depression but helped me through the dark times of both

The Outrun - Amy Liptrot
The Nix - Nathan Hill
The Argonauts - Maggie Nelson

Bluets - Maggie Nelson

All At Sea - Decca Aitkenhead

A Little Life - Hanya Yanigahara (take care with this one though)

Let The Great World Spin - Colum McCann

Harry Potter Series - JK Rowling

Fates and Furies - Lauren Groff

The Amazing Adventures Kavalier and Clay - Michael Chabon

Jonathan Livingston Seagull - Richard Bach

Goodnight Mr Tom - Michelle Magorian

H is for Hawk - Helen MacDonald

White Teeth - Zadie Smith

Song of Achilles - Madeline Miller

Swell - Jenny Landreth

Special Topics in Calamity Physics - Marisha Pessel

With massive thanks to our patrons...

Rachael Chadwick

Nicole Larkin

Rebecca Hunter

Fiona Garnsworthy

Izzy Kennedy

Gem Morson

Luc De Brouwer

Aileen Rice-Jones

Sophie Trew

Tracie Gledhill

Michaela Twite

Joanna Forest

Fleur Elliott

Josie Bramhall

Jackie Newton

Carly Little

Marta Cooper

Kate Heathman

Ciara McCrory

Jenny Baker

Sue Walker

Jane Tasker

Kate Bolton

Pedro Ribeiro

Jeannie Bee

Caroline Matthews

Samantha Vine

Andrew Mitchell & Andrew Carswell

James & Elizabeth Alderson

Becci Hammond

Gary Wilmot MBE

Jayne Little

Sarah Firmston

Briony Langley-Miles

Fawzia King

Carol Wilmot

Lizzie & Francisco Carballo Sells

Sarah McLoughlin

Lottie Sheppard

Louise Clarke

Charlotte Soman

Lucy Aerts

Judi Asquith

Louisa Collington

Hollie Jones

Sinead Molloy

The Ridges

Vix Ross

Alison & Andrew Purkiss

Emily Coleman-Boyle

Ross Brotherston

Aggie Bainbridge

Sarah Hedges

Jessica Sumerling

Em Eustice

Jackie Scully

Kay Ross

Sandra Connolly & Adam Harris

Beryl Richards

Jill Bramhall

Alex Bosier

Fiona McDonnell

Anthea Christie

Charlotte Taylor

Jane Mark

JP Jones

Rosie Hoare

Nicola Carr

Victoria Leyton

The Hawthornthwaites

Claire Norman

Holly Worthington

Jess Rose

Sara Purkiss-Ayre

Dee Brotherston

Alex Freer

Jessica Hurley

Pam Cowburn

Jo Miller

Susannah Wilson

Alison & Pete Cooke

Jane Bagnall

Evelyn Mackinnon-Morrow

Emma & Andrew Sherboyd

Lucinda "Theroux" Mabbitt

Alison Tonkin

Jess Read

Barbara Brandley

Vikki Norman

Paul Lewis

Michael McCann

Kim & Andre Dorset

Julie Robertson

Jenny Matthews

Humberto de Sousa

Zeus Kanji

Rachel Molina

Caroline Saunders

Helen Skehens

Ceri Jones

Amy Hampshire

Lizzie Penny

Helen Skinner

Kate Lester

Francesca Howard

Shirley Judd

Harriet Matheson

Jane Jones

Danny Denhard

Sian Evans

Ann-Marie Stevenson

Tania Harrison

Natasha Schmidt

Katherine Page

Nicky Eldon

Sophie Dopierala

Alice Judge-Talbot

Sarah Capper

Jaclyn Ruth Craig

Kathryn Alderson

Duncan Jennings

Kirsty Clegg

Amy Jenner

Laura Derryman-Warren

Anna Rainbow

Amy Howarth

Emma Fisher

Sam Fleet

Peter & Shirley Jones

Alexandra Brown

Karen Hobbs

Marina McKeever

Emily Hodge

Liz Williams

Charlotte Green

Ashley Wood

Helen W

Kayla Jones

Annie Varrall

Tilly Varrall

Hilary Ashman

Bronya Glett

Amy Sheppard

Francesca Jones

Lauren Mahon

Jayne Rudd

Luke Johnson

Hannah Dell

Maddy Grant

Victoria J Fode

Martin Block

Kathryn Newman

Sue Newman

Dawn Warren

Marian Ellis

Ross & Nerys Mitchell

Hannah Livesey

Kara Rennie

Emily English

Lucy Hardy

Sally Lovett

Gillian Lawrence

Lindy H

Louise Jopling

Liz Newman

LuLu Socratous

Sara Boomsma

Ralph Stokeld

Danny Masters

Stacey Fenton

Vicki Norman

Nikki D

Rach Moss

Ben W

"Groovy"

Jane Hunter Walsh

Brian Curran